Atlantis

Atlantis

✦

The Origin of a Legend

Greg Alexander

iUniverse, Inc.

New York Lincoln Shanghai

Atlantis
The Origin of a Legend

iUniverse, Inc.

For information address:
iUniverse, Inc.
2021 Pine Lake Road, Suite 100
Lincoln, NE 68512
www.iuniverse.com

ISBN: 0-595-33267-6 (pbk)
ISBN: 0-595-66804-6 (cloth)

Printed in the United States of America

Contents

Atlantis, Old and New

Ever since Plato's account of the story in the Timaeus and Critias in the 4th century B.C., there has been an enduring fascination with the island civilisation called Atlantis. The possibility that such an ancient civilisation had at one time existed appears to explain man's sudden development from hunter-gatherer to metal worker and the builder of cities. Indeed, if such a place as Atlantis had ever existed it might even be described as having been the birthplace of civilisation, the point from where all human technological achievement has advanced.

However, was the story told by Plato in any way based upon fact—or was it purely fable? Modern archaeology prevails towards the view that human development took place gradually and can best be considered as a process of evolution. The evidence does not suggest that civilisation was handed to men by a superior race but was instead discovered over a period of time, piecemeal. When one group of peoples made a technological breakthrough, others quickly followed. It would appear, therefore, that technology spread throughout the various parts of the globe by way of social interactions between the peoples concerned.

But, such a view, although open-ended and pragmatic, still leaves a possibility that such technological developments originated from a common focus in the first place. When one considers the vast period of time covered by the stone age, and also the correspondingly vast period covered by the iron age, isn't it a wonder that man was able to bridge such a gap at all? Having worked with copper and bronze, it was inevitable that he would soon develop the technology to work with iron also. But what a leap it must have been between shaping pieces of flint and smelting metal? Did such a development come about quite by chance and then spread like wildfire throughout the Near East and

Europe? Indeed, the possibility that such advances originated from a common source has surely to be borne in mind, even though proof that might indicate this has so far been lacking? The eras of the Late Neolithic and Bronze Ages still remain periods of mystery and legend, and with all the uncertainties, who is to say what the case actually was at the end of the day?

Also across the globe there are many examples of parallel legends that speak of wise men or superior peoples who gave the gifts of civilisation to their forebears. Such legends, although at first reinforcing the story, also at the same time tend to cast doubt upon its originality. Perhaps the tale is little more than a product of man's unconscious and represents his continual desire for an explanation as to how things came to be? Moreover, we can never be absolutely certain as to how accurate any of the details that Plato gives us about the Atlantis story itself actually are, and it is this point which is critical in answering the question as to the story's reality. Or, to put it slightly differently, in spite of the theoretical possibilities as to the story's truth, if the historical details are incorrect or inaccurate, then the story is pure fable.

Indeed, some have even questioned whether the story of such a lost island was ever current in the classical world at all and whether the story was not purely a creation on Plato's part. It appears from this author's writings that he was very much in the habit of creating the odd fictitious situation now and then in order to demonstrate a particular philosophical point. In the Timaeus and Critias the point in question had been how exactly would an ideal society be constituted? Because of this we can only speculate that Plato had perhaps elaborated upon a pre-existing story to make the society in question seem that little more advanced than it really was. Indeed, in his account many of the facts do show evidence of at least some exaggeration and we are left wondering how the constructions that he spoke of could ever have been accomplished even in the classical era, let alone at the time claimed of 10,000 B.C. If much of the story had indeed been Plato's own creation, a result of his having embellished a story that was already in circulation at the time, then how much of it exactly was authentic? This, of course, is entirely open to debate and such a question can only properly be addressed after an appropriate examination of all the possible sources.

Another author who also makes a passing mention of the story of Atlantis is Plutarch. In his famed account of the life of Solon he mentions that the latter had been planning a lengthy poem on the subject. Indeed, it was from Solon, through the intermediation of a great grandfather, that Plato had also come by the story. However, it appears that to a large extent Plutarch had been entirely reliant on Plato in his detailing of this particular fact and even mentions the philosopher by name. In spite of this, Plutarch's comments on Plato's account are rather informative as he describes the author as having created "an elaborate masterpiece…as if it were the site on some fine estate." It appears therefore that Plutarch had also been suspicious of the fact that Plato had perhaps been rather too imaginative in his re-telling of the story. The author also tells us that Solon had never quite finished his poem due to the onset of old age. Whether this was true or not, no fragment of the poem has ever been retrieved. Indeed, Plato himself left his most detailed account in the Critias in an incomplete state, probably for the same reasons.

The only other classical author apart from Plato to make any real significant mention of the story of Atlantis was Diodorus Siculus. This particular author, however, does not actually discuss the island itself but rather its inhabitants—the Atlantians. It was the latter who apparently fought a number of battles against their closest rivals, the Amazons. Indeed they had their work cut out because it was the Amazons who, according to Diodorus, were also to challenge the might of Greece as they swept through much of Asia Minor. The account of Diodorus differs significantly from that of Plato in that the Atlantians are a rather nondescript group of people on the whole who have no other claim to fame than their rivalry with the all-female tribe.

Diodorus does, however, go on to state that the Atlantians at one time had control over a vast swathe of the African continent.

But in spite of all these uncertainties, it has always been tempting to recognise the possibility that an advanced civilisation had perhaps existed in very ancient times—a civilisation that had been destroyed by some cataclysmic event. Because of the important position classical literature held for many years in the educated world, it had always been the opinion that there was indeed truth to the fable. Indeed, why should such a learned people as the Greeks have even made mention of such a thing if there was no substance to it whatsoever? Perhaps this once mighty continent had been destroyed by the Great Flood itself? Indeed one can only imagine how the story was reinforced by the Biblical account of the Destruction of Eden, as the parallels are only too obvious.

With the exploration of the New World in the 16th century, the suggestion was made that perhaps America had been the long lost continent. It itself is surrounded by an ocean, the Atlantic, which has to be navigated in order to arrive there. Indeed when the European explorers had first arrived in the New World, strange people were encountered speaking an unknown language and with peculiar customs. Had these been the original inhabitants of Atlantis? Moreover the conquistadors had also encountered a people called the Aztecs who coincidently had claimed that they had come from a mysterious land called 'Aztlan' which made them sound even more like the inhabitants of the lost continent. To the Spanish explorers, the customs of these people seemed barbaric and drew an easy comparison with the bloodthirsty rites described by Plato which took place on Atlantis.

Exploration of the surrounding jungle produced further evidence that they were dealing with a lost civilisation. Hidden in the surrounding jungle were the now ruined buildings of the ancient Maya. These stepped structures, rather like the pyramids of Giza, ascended towards the skies, towering above the surrounding undergrowth. Images of strange beings adorned their walls and portrayals of gruesome sacrifices were also found. Truly, a lost civilisation had been encountered, but was it the same as the one described by Plato? The only apparent difference was that these buildings were still standing and had not been destroyed in some cataclysmic event.

Such discoveries only fermented the imaginations of the conquistadors still further and stories began to circulate of the legendary city called El Dorado. The latter was said to have been fabulously rich in gold such that its very walls were hung with the stuff. The gold the Spanish had already obtained from among the local populace was enough to convince them that the land was comparatively rich in the mineral. Were even better discoveries awaiting them in this respect? Needless to say, despite a number of quests to find it, El Dorado proved elusive and, even though it is easy to say in retrospect, had probably never existed in the first place. The more likely explanation is that its name, which means 'the gilded one', referred to a custom held by one of the tribes of daily sprinkling their chieftain from head to foot in gold dust. At the end of the day the chief would bathe himself in a sacred lake to clean himself off.

In more recent times a further explanation of the story of Atlantis has come to the fore in the shape of the island of Santorini, some miles to the north of Crete. The latter was subject to a huge volcanic explosion in the fifteenth century B.C. which almost completely destroyed the island, leaving a huge caldera crater. Crete itself was also significantly affected by the resultant ash fall and tidal waves, and there is much archaeological evidence to suggest that the east part of the island suffered extensive devastation. The Minoan civilisation based upon both these islands also appears to have significantly dwindled around this time, suggesting that a large part of the island had become uninhabitable. Not long after the eruption, Mycenaean settlers from the mainland began to invade the island.

As for the extent of the eruption which destroyed Santorini, estimates have placed it as four times more powerful than that of Krakatoa. This island volcano, to the west of Java, which erupted in 1883, sent huge dust clouds over twenty miles into the atmosphere which were the cause of brilliant red sunsets over the entire globe for the next few years. The explosion itself was heard over three thousand miles away in Western Australia and forty metre tidal waves affected many areas. One of these waves swept an anchored warship over two miles inland.

Like Krakatoa, Mount Thera, as it was called in ancient times, lies along one of the Earth's fault lines and would have been affected by several years of earthquakes prior to the final devastating eruption. In many respects the destruction of Santorini and parts of Crete is extremely reminiscent of the story of Atlantis. Crete itself was the home of an ancient civilisation which was comparatively advanced for its time and which had its heyday prior to the rise of Hellenic Greece. The Minoans were of such a sophistication that they had developed their own system of writing and counting which would be of such an influence later on on the mainland. Because they dwelt on an island they were also a seafaring people who had many contacts around the Mediterranean, including Egypt.

Were these the people Plato had been thinking of when he had described his ideal civilisation in the Timaeus? All that really differs is the precise geographical location of the island. In Plato the lost continent lay at the very heart of the Atlantic Ocean 'beyond the Pillars of Heracles' whereas Crete, of course, is quite clearly contained within the same sea that surrounds the coastline of mainland Greece. Another objection which can be raised is that the decline of the Minoan civilisation was far from sudden but took place over a distinct period of time, as the archaeological evidence appears to suggest. However, it is almost certain that the eruption on Santorini had been the cause of this decline.

Due to the fact that the Minoans had flourished many years before the rise of Hellenic Greece, the ancient civilisation was also the subject of many myths and legends among the Greeks themselves. According to these legends, the island had been ruled by a King Minos, after whom incidentally the civilisation had been named, who ordered the construction of many fine buildings within his domain. One of these was the Labyrinth, an extremely complex building that his chief architect Daedalus had constructed. Within its myriad of walls, the Minotaur was imprisoned, who, according to story, happened to be the king's son who had been born half man, half bull. The story goes that the creature required regular human sacrifice until the hero Theseus slew him, escaping from the maze with the help of the king's daughter Ariadne.

Some have suggested that the Palace of Knossos, the remains of which are located towards the centre of the island, represents the building that the legend of the Labyrinth refers to. The palace consisted of scores of rooms with many passageways linking them together giving its ground plan a rather maze-like quality. In some of these rooms the image of a pair of bull's horns is frequently depicted on the walls in addition to columns which may at one time have been the site at which offerings were made. It is thought that a bull cult may have existed at the island where the animal was slaughtered according to a rather gruesome ritual. Although there are many examples of bull cults in the ancient world, the evidence that one had existed on Crete in Minoan times is slim. The main factor that has led many to form this opinion is the legend of the Minotaur itself, or alternatively the 'Minoan bull'. But whatever the case, however, it appears that cult temples were never actually built by the Minoans, and that the various areas at which offerings were made were contained within the already existing palaces or houses.

Such a bull sacrifice is also found in Plato's account of Atlantis where the animal is offered at the temple of Poseidon located at the centre of the island's capital. According to the account, after the various officials who governed the island had gathered, the animal was slaughtered and its blood collected and sprinkled over the top of a column. Had such ceremonies also taken place at the Palace of Knossos? Within the latter, rooms containing columns have also been uncovered, such as in the basement of the palace. Had bulls been kept here ready for sacrificial offering? Certainly, the excavator of Knossos, Sir Arthur Evans, was of the opinion that offerings could well have been performed within certain areas of the palace—but opinion remains divided on this issue.

The other main theme raised by the Atlantis story is that of cataclysmic events in the distant past which shaped the future history of mankind. Across the globe there are many parallel myths and legends of such destructive events, but there is little evidence to suggest these phenomena were ever more than localised phenomena. Inevitably widespread flooding or earthquakes would have occurred in the past within certain regions of the globe which would have led to a correspondingly high death toll among the local populace and the story of these events would have been recorded in the form of myths and legends. But was it possible that an entire island or even a continent could simply have sunk into the sea during the course of an event like this, disappearing without trace? Surely such an event would have left its mark somewhere upon the surface of the globe which would be only too obvious for a modern day geologist to spot?

Indeed along the entire length of the mid-Atlantic a volcanic fault is indeed found, but nowhere along its course is there evidence of widespread land slippage. Was it possible that such a fault could simply have opened up sometime in the distant past and swallowed an entire island without leaving a trace? Such an event would seem unlikely, based upon our present understanding of geological processes, and would surely have been accompanied by widespread volcanic activity? Perhaps the event was far more isolated and involved a volcanic island which simply detonated, leaving little evidence of its prior existence, a possibility which has been examined already. However, there is a third possibility that would certainly have produced enough local devastation to destroy an island and would also have produced effects noticeable across the entire globe—an impact with an astronomical body.

It is the case that if an asteroid of appreciable dimensions, such as one of several kilometres across for example, or even a small comet, impacted with the Earth, the results would be utter devastation over a wide area. Such an event involving a large asteroid is thought to have taken place sometime towards the end of the Cretaceous Era which resulted in the extinction of the dinosaurs. Scientists inform us that such an impact would have led to climatic changes on a global scale and would have left a crater of significant proportions. Such a crater, thought to have been caused by the asteroid responsible for this extinction, is found in the shape of the Chicxulub Basin at the Yucatan Peninsula, Central America. It is over 300km wide and was formed during the period in question, that is, 65 million years ago. Drilling samples taken from the basin indicate that it is meteoritic in origin. Coincidently, the Yucatan Peninsula was also the place where the ancient Maya were to arrive and settle, but by the time they had arrived the sides of the crater would already have been significantly eroded.

If such an event had indeed taken place towards the end of the Cretaceous Era, is it possible that such an event had also occurred sometime during human history which had perhaps been the cause of the disappearance of an entire island? One famous example of an impact crater is found at Barringer, Arizona. It is over a kilometre across and almost 200 meters deep and was formed some 50,000 years ago. Even though this is well within the historical epoch of early man, this is well before 10,000 B.C., the time when Atlantis was said to have been destroyed. A far more recent event, and again thought to have been caused by a meteoritic explosion, occurred in 1908 over the Tunguska River in Siberia. Trees were burnt and flattened within a twenty-mile radius, almost as if a nuclear bomb had been detonated over the site. Such is the awesome power of nature.

Indeed in Plato's account of the Atlantis story, the suggestion is clearly made that a world-changing event had been the cause of the island's destruction. The Egyptian priest in Sais who had related the story, had also claimed that there had been a number of cataclysmic events in the course of human history, only one of which had been responsible for the destruction of Atlantis. As an example he mentions the Greek story of how Phaëthon had taken his father's chariot and steered the sun from its place in the sky such that it had scorched the earth, claiming that the Egyptians had knowledge of many other such world changing events. The Egyptian was of the opinion that such events occur periodically as a result of the cyclical nature of the movements of the heavens. After the completion of such a cycle, fire, in the form of a savage drought or water, in the form of a huge deluge, wreaks havoc and destruction upon the Earth.

Could such cycles be found in the planetary perturbations of the asteroid belt which cause these rocky bodies to be steered in an Earthward direction? In recent years we have been made far more aware of the possibility of such an astronomical bombardment after the collision of the comet Shoemaker-Levy 9 with Jupiter. The impact caused huge gaping holes to appear in the side of the gaseous planet. If such a collision had occurred with the Earth it would surely mean the end of civilisation as we know it? Perhaps as a consequence of this it is worth paying heed to the story of Atlantis and that it is not impossible for world-changing events to occur at times with devastating results.

1

Plato's Account in the Timaeus and Critias

Before his death in 348 B.C., the Timaeus is one of the last works to be authored by Plato. It takes the form of a dialogue and, as is always the case with his writings, his chief mentor, Socrates, is a leading speaker. The discussion is apparently continued from the previous day and concerns what precisely constitutes an 'ideal state'. This topic had also formed the basis of the Republic, Plato's most important and certainly most extensive work written down some twenty years earlier.

After an introductory discussion on the ordering of such a state, a second speaker, Critias, who happened to be Plato's maternal great grandfather, considers it informative to relate a story that he had heard from his own grandfather. Apparently the latter had in turn been told the story by his father, Dropides, who had been a friend of the great and wise Solon. This individual, himself one of the founders of the Athenian constitution, had originally heard of the story via an Egyptian priest while staying at Sais. It recounted one of the great victories the city of Athens had won over her enemies in the distant past. Solon had received the story while discussing with the Egyptians their many records of the past, the collection of which, so they claimed, were far more extensive than those held by the Greeks. The explanation they gave for this latter fact being that in the past there had been a number of great catastrophes, but due to the peculiar circumstances that are found in the Nile valley, their own civilisation had survived each of these. The priest stated that prior to the last of these great catastrophes which involved a huge deluge, Athens had been second to none in both power and influence.

The priest then proceeded to relate a series of events that he claimed had occurred some 9,000 years ago. At this point in time Athens was just beginning to prosper under the guidance of its tutelary goddess when a power from the Atlantic threatened the entire safety of the city. The race in question inhabited an island situated within the Atlantic directly opposite the Pillars of Heracles. The island was of vast proportions and was more of a continent therefore, being greater in size than 'both Libya and Asia combined'. Being both bountiful and prosperous, the island supported a powerful nation which had already gained control over a large part of North Africa and was now attempting to gain control of Europe as well. The Athenians, renowned for their bravery, were determined to stop this people in their tracks. The latter fought hard and long with the Atlantians and liberated many of the lands they had conquered. At last the men of Athens advanced upon the island itself but it was suddenly besieged by a series of earthquakes. In conclusion, the story teller relates, the entire island sank into the sea during the course of just one day, taking many of the fighting soldiers with it.

So ends Plato's account of the story as given in the Timaeus. The next account, that of the Critias, is, as its title suggests, a continuation of that commenced in the Timaeus as it shares the same speaker. The second dialogue gives a far more detailed description of the precise nature of the island and especially of the character of its capital city.

According to Plato, when the lands of Earth had been apportioned by the immortals, Athena and Hephaestos had received the lands of Greece while Poseidon was allotted the island of Atlantis. Towards the middle of the island, at the centre of a vast plain, a small hill was located on which had dwelt Evenor and his wife Leucippe, along with their daughter Cleito. Poseidon took the latter as his wife and she bore him five sets of male twins. The hill in question on which the two had met was then enclosed by Poseidon with three concentric rings of water and two of land. Also upon the hill were found two springs, one of which was hot, the other cold, and this watered the soil, causing much abundant growth.

Poseidon then commenced to apportion the entire island between each of his ten sons which he made king over each allotment. Atlas, the eldest, and from whom the island eventually derived its name, was given the land containing the very place where he was born and which would become the site of the future capital city. His younger brother Gadirus received the land on the side nearest the Pillars of Heracles, while the four other pairs, Ampheres and Euaemon, Mneseus and Autochthon, Elasippus and Mestor, and Azaes and Diaprepes had the remaining land divided equally among them.

The line of kings to follow Atlas were particularly prosperous, their wealth deriving both from the island's natural mineral resources and their many trading links built up as a direct result of the island's power and influence abroad. One metal the island was particularly rich in was that of orichalc which now, of course, is only known by name but which at the time was considered as more precious than gold. The island was also the place of habitation for many exotic plants and animals including elephants, topical fruits and incense bearing trees.

As for the capital city, a palace was first built upon the hill and a bridge across the rings of water was also constructed. The royal residence was of great splendour and was constructed using the costliest of materials. From the rings of water an enormous canal was dug leading directly to the sea, turning the entire city into a convenient inland harbour. The canal was some three hundred feet wide, a hundred feet deep and ran for some six miles from the city to the coast. Surrounding the citadel and its concentric rings, three huge walls were built equipped with towers and gates that guarded each of the bridges over the circles of water. The stone for these walls had been quarried from the central island, which itself had a diameter of almost a mile, and the cuttings that were left were then used as docks being naturally roofed above by the very rock itself. The wall around the outermost ring was encased in bronze and the wall around the inner ring was covered with tin, while that around the citadel itself, the precious orichalc was used which glowed vividly in the sun.

Immediately adjacent to the royal residence on the central hill, the temple and shrine of Poseidon was found. The shrine marked the very spot where the ten kings of Atlantis had been born and was surrounded by an impregnable wall shaped from solid gold. Each of the ten kings visited this place every year to give their respects. Poseidon's temple immediately beside it was both generously proportioned and lavishly decorated. Its outer walls were covered from top to bottom in silver and the inner walls, floor and columns were covered in glistening orichalc. The ceiling was formed of solid ivory and studded with each of the precious metals. All of the statues that were both in and outside of the temple were of solid gold and depicted such things as the Nereids riding on dolphins and each of the ten kings accompanied by their wives. The hot and cold springs that flowed from the side of the hill, were fed into open air pools and hot baths, and were also used to supply both the royal residence and to water the grove of Poseidon.

The concentric rings of land surrounding the citadel were also used for a number of quite varied purposes. For example there were several further temples as well as gardens for relaxing in. On the inner of these islands a race course was found which followed the entire circumference of the tract of land. The soldiers' quarters were also located upon one of these island rings, their function being there to protect both the safety of the city and the king. The waterways between the islands also served as the docking for many triremes.

There was a further wall surrounding the entire city at a distance of some six miles or so from the outer waterway. It started at the mouth of the canal where it joined the sea and continued right round in a full circle, arriving at the sea again on the opposite side of the canal. Within this wall the housing of the city's populace was located and within the canal hordes of merchant ships were gathered ready to embark on their many trading missions.

As for the rest of the island, the terrain was decidedly mountainous and the land at the coasts ended abruptly at the sea. On the south side of the island, however, was a large plain of rectangular form which again was surrounded on all sides by mountains. It covered an area of 300 miles by 200 miles and at its centre towards the sea stood the city. On the slopes of the mountains surrounding the plain, many villages were found that thrived upon the fertile slopes.

Enclosing the plain was a huge man-made ditch of over a stade in width (a stade being about six hundred feet) which received all the water that flowed from the mountainside. From this ditch further canals were cut to fully irrigate the soils of the plain within. Ultimately the water from the ditch fed into the waterways surrounding the city and also to the main canal which led to the sea. The whole system could be used to float timber as well as the yearly harvest from the mountains to the city, ready for further transportation as required.

The plain itself was divided into a number of allotments, each covering an area of ten square stades. The holders of these were expected to supply a single soldier and in all there were 60,000 allotments. The villages within the mountains were also able to supply a large quantity of soldiers if necessary, these latter units being led by the holders of the allotments. Each regular infantryman was also obliged to supply one sixth of a war chariot complete with all its equipment.

The ten kings who ruled Atlantis each held sovereign power in that part of the island which had been granted them by Poseidon. However, the kings also ruled according to a mutual agreement which had been enshrined in law by Poseidon himself. The contents of this law was engraved upon a column of pure orichalc located within his temple, and every six years the ten kings would meet at the temple to swear an oath of allegiance to it. They did this by offering a single bull as a sacrifice to Poseidon and, according to the custom, the blood of the bull was then poured over the top of the column on which the law was engraved. Each of the ten kings then drank in turn from a cup containing some of this blood.

Due to the island's success, it grew ever wealthier and its citizens enjoyed all the benefits accompanying such prosperity. However, as a consequence of their ease of living, they became rather too inclined to pleasure and their hard work and endeavour soon gave way to indulgence and excess. Inevitably, such behaviour did not go unnoticed by the immortals and Zeus himself eventually stepped in to take action. He summoned all of the gods together on Mount Olympus where a judgement was pronounced upon the inhabitants of the island. When the conference had been concluded the immortals unleashed their wrath upon the inhabitants and in the course of a single day the entire island sank into the sea.

So ends Plato's account of the story of Atlantis as described in the Critias, if not rather abruptly. It appears that the author never actually completed the entire dialogue and the point at which he chose to end just so happens to be towards the very conclusion of the speaker's account of the lost continent. In all, the story was told so as to both entertain and to impress upon its listeners the skill and design that had gone into the construction of the city. A new kind of society is also hinted at, but whether it represented an ideal one is, at the end of the day, open to debate. The ignominious fate of the islanders at the very end of the story rather suggests that it wasn't, but the account still offers an interesting example of a society ordered along slightly differing lines.

One enigma immediately raised by the account given in the Critias, is what was the precise identity of the metal called 'orichalc'? The other metals, such as gold, silver, bronze and tin, are all quite clearly mentioned by name elsewhere in the story, so we are at an apparent loss in identifying it. Certainly, it appears that the metal was considered as precious and also gleamed or glistened brightly in the sun, but what metal could this have been other than gold or silver? It is difficult to believe that the metal concerned was iron, as the latter tends to tarnish and in any case we have no reason to believe that the culture in question was actually living in the Iron Age. Another possibility however is that the metal was copper. Although soft, copper in colour tends to glow with the 'fire-like' quality mentioned in the text. It is also the case that this particular metal was discovered very early on by man, many societies having used it immediately prior to the Bronze Age.

Had it been the case that orichalc was copper? The name 'orichalc' itself is of interest as it is apparently derived from a separate Latin and a Greek word put together. The first syllable 'ori' happens to be a common shortening for the Latin 'aurum' meaning gold. The second, 'chalc', is a shortening of 'chalkedon', the Greek for precious stone. It would appear, therefore, that the name *orichalc*, when translated literally, would mean a 'golden coloured stone'. But this is peculiar, for why should a metal be described as a stone? This is not so difficult to understand, however, if it is considered that orichalc had perhaps been the first metal to be discovered. The first metal to be discovered immediately prior to the Bronze Age, of course, was copper. And the metal could also be described as having gold-like qualities to its colouration. When Plato used the compound word 'orichalc', therefore, in his account of the story, had he in fact been trying to say 'the first metal ever to be discovered'?

Indeed copper was in fact the first metal to be used by man as a result of its being found in its natural state close to the surface of the earth and can also be very easily hammered into shape. In the Near East it was used as early as 8,000 B.C. However, it was not until sometime later, around 3,500 B.C., that it was actually learnt how to melt it in the presence of arsenic to create bronze, and not long after that how to alloy it with tin to make the same metal. Knowing these dates, is it possible that a metal such as 'orichalc', if its supply had been abundant enough, could have been used by man as early as 9,500 B.C.? Such a scenario must surely be a possibility, especially if we are dealing with a so far undiscovered lost civilisation.

So if this was the case, then what of the use of gold, silver and bronze that is also mentioned by Plato? If the metals had indeed been worked with by the inhabitants of the island, then this would place the civilisation far later than 9,500 B.C. The first recorded use of gold, for instance, is around 3,500 B.C., and for silver, 2,400 B.C. Perhaps the islander's supposed use was merely a literary embellishment on Plato's part and, in fact, there is some evidence in the various details of the story that might suggest that such had been the case—but we will be coming to this issue later on in the chapter. Certainly, ironworking is mentioned as having taken place on the island, so perhaps it is safe to assume that the society in question was right at the beginning of pre-iron age, that is around 1,000 B.C. This last date, even as a bare minimum, is itself of great antiquity and places it well before the beginning of much of recorded history. In fact, the Bronze Age in general is an era of myth, magic and legend, the various historical happenings of this period being handed down to us in story form.

Having established the possibility that metal-working societies could indeed have existed in such ancient times, the question still remains that the number of years quoted prior to Solon in which these events were said to have occurred were in fact inaccurate or misleading and were not actually 9,000 in number at all. It is known that the Egyptians followed the custom of dividing the year into three separate seasons, that of the time of the Nile inundation, and spring and the harvest; the actual beginning and the end of the year being marked by the heliacal rising of the dog star Sirius. However, it is also known that in some of their records the passing of time is not measured in years at all but in the number of important events or festivals that occurred in that year. Could it have been the case that the number 9,000 quoted by the Egyptian priest actually referred to, say, for example, the number of seasons that had passed by since that time? If this had been so, and as there are of course three such seasons in each year, this would make the actual date of the destruction of Atlantis sometime around 3,500 B.C.

Of course, this is an entirely different figure, but perhaps one that is also far more realistic at the end of the day. At this particular point in time bronze would have been a comparatively new invention and gold was just beginning to be produced, so it is not an unfair suggestion that a comparatively advanced civilisation had already established itself in this respect and was even leading the way. Perhaps the reason why the society in question had been so advanced in this respect was entirely due to the plentiful supply of orichalc at their disposal, which, as we have suggested, could have been copper, and which might also have encouraged their further experimentation with the working of metal.

Again, a date of circa 3,500 B.C. is very much in the distant and forgotten past and is even prior to the Mycenaean and Minoan cultures. At this time Greece was still in the Neolithic Period and the Egyptians had not yet embarked upon their long marriage with civilisation. But if this had been the era when this lost civilisation had flourished, then how could it have happened that Stone Age Greece had successfully managed to repulse a technically superior race? Perhaps their exceptional bravery against the Atlantians had proved sufficient and that sling shot and flint arrowheads were just as effective when appropriately used against the superior bronze weapons? Such a scenario is indeed possible, but what had actually been the case will have to remain an open question for the time being.

Indeed, a date of 3,500 B.C. would also place the story as contemporary with pre-dynastic Egypt, which is before the very first of the founding pharaohs of the Old Kingdom. It is considered that the first pharaoh, Menes, whose own precise history is clouded in mystery, ruled sometime around 3,000 B.C. Is it possible, therefore, that the records the Egyptian priest was referring to, dated back to this period? Perhaps the records had made mention of past battles between the inhabitants of Egypt and the Atlantians and the subsequent defeat of the latter at the hands of the Greeks? These events of course would have transpired in Egyptian prehistory and then passed on by word of mouth in story form. In fact, such a picture is fairly plausible and it is perhaps now possible to understand the Egyptian's remark that their records were far more ancient than those of the Greeks who were 'young by comparison'. Hieroglyphic texts have indeed been found in Egypt which date back to circa 3,000 B.C. whereas in Greece the earliest records that they have date to around the seventh century B.C. Of course, this would make the Egyptian records vastly more ancient by comparison.

That the Atlantis story referred to some actual historical reality is far easier to comprehend when we accept the possible correctness of such a scenario. Even if the details of the story had been embellished over many years of retelling, even by Plato himself, at least we can recognise at least some original substance to the story. How accurate the surviving details of the story exactly are of course and what historical events the story actually referred to, is a matter which can only be fully answered as the book progresses.

One particular topic of immediate interest is the precise nature of the island itself. According to Plato, the island was comprised of extremely mountainous terrain, even precipitously so, for he says that the very sides of these mountains finished abruptly at the sea. Apparently the only level area to be found on the island was the rectangular plain towards its south where the city was built. But even this was apparently surrounded by steep-sided mountains and which, so it was stated, offered the plain shelter from buffeting north winds. Plato also tells us that the mountains in this latter range were higher than any other found in the known world at the time. Indeed it was as a result of this precipitous aspect of the island that many of its inhabitants were forced to dwell high upon the slopes many feet above sea-level. Raised valleys within these ranges afforded the kings who ruled in these parts the appropriate comfort and security along with fertile soils for farming.

But one unavoidable objection that must be raised about the island's geography in this respect is how such an island-continent the size of 'Libya and Asia combined', could have been so mountainous throughout? Surely such a situation would be completely impossible? All that we can assume is that the story, at least in part, had been exaggerated by Plato. This leads us to conclude that either the land mass called Atlantis was actually far smaller, making it more of an island as such than a continent, or that the land was not entirely mountainous throughout but only in certain parts where tall ranges were found. This leaves us with two distinctly different pictures of the land mass in question. In the first instance Atlantis is a small but highly mountainous island along the lines of the equivalents found in the Pacific; in the second instance it is a large continent containing mountain ranges which just so happen to surround a rectangular plain towards its south side. But which is the correct picture?

A second interesting feature about the island is the fact that hot springs occurred upon it which would appear to indicate the presence of volcanic activity. Had the land mass been located over one of the earth's many geological fault lines? Perhaps it had been the very fault line which runs the entire length of the Atlantic Ocean as, according to Plato, the island had been situated at the very heart of this expanse of water? Indeed, had it been this fact that had led to the island's eventual destruction in a series of monumental earthquakes? If the island had been so located, then it is also possible that the island had been formed as a result of the same process, that the island was volcanic in origin. Such islands are inherently unstable and are prone to eruptions and on some rare occasions, complete destruction.

If the island's geological history had been so constituted, then it is more than likely that the land mass involved had been a medium sized island rather than a continent. Perhaps such an origin could also explain why its terrain was so mountainous throughout and why the sides of the island ended so steeply at the sea? Indeed such physical features are often the case with volcanic islands, the Pacific Ocean offering many such examples. These islands are often rich in vegetation, supporting many varied life forms, the rich green growth clinging to their steep sloping sides. In this particular respect they very much take the form of island paradises. Indeed it is often the case that man also has made his home on these islands having voyaged there many years previously by boat. Such a scenario must surely be a temptation especially when it is considered that the island may not have been that far from the Tropics which would have given it a comparatively warm climate. Such a climate would also have meant that the island would have been capable of supporting the exotic life forms mentioned by Plato.

The exact location of the hot springs mentioned is the cause of a further reflection as Plato informs us that they were present upon the very hill on which the capital city was built. Is it possible therefore that this hill had also been volcanic in origin? It would appear that it must have been, though the hill in question is only described as having been small in size. Indeed how could one make such a bold suggestion as that the inhabitants had built their most important city upon the cone of a still active volcano? Surely such an eventuality would have been ludicrous, especially if the volcano in question was still growing? But what other explanation is there for the presence of hot springs upon a hilly prominence which, according to the description, is surrounded by the flat expanse of a plain? We will return to this point at the end of the chapter when we discuss the destruction of Atlantis.

The next aspect of the account worthy of discussion is the precise nature of the buildings present in its chief city. Although Plato does not exactly go into lavish detail in his description of them, from the detail that he does reveal it is obvious that their architecture is very Greek in character. For example Poseidon's temple followed a very classical format. At the front of the rectangular shaped building a pediment was found containing various carved figures that in turn was supported by columns. Rows of the latter were also found inside the building supporting the ceiling. Within the temple a cult image of Poseidon was located which again follows the Greek custom. Outside of the temple, within the confines of its precinct, stood an altar, and not far from this a grove dedicated to the island's founder. Indeed, if one had encountered such an arrangement in the city of Athens itself it would not have looked out of place in the slightest. All that really set it apart at the end of the day was the lavish amounts of silver and orichalc that had been used in covering the buildings walls.

Had this temple originally been Greek in style—or was it purely a literary creation on Plato's part? If it had been then it would appear that the civilisation in question had more likely been Minoan and the island therefore Crete. But as mentioned earlier, the Minoans were not in the habit of constructing temple buildings as were the Greeks and the island of Crete is relatively devoid of such structures, that is, apart from the later building activities of the Greeks themselves when they eventually gained control of the island. Alternatively, perhaps it could be suggested that the building on Atlantis represented a prototype of the later classical architecture? Due to the influence this island civilisation had upon the Greeks, the latter had perhaps copied their style of building? Indeed, such appears to have been the situation as far as Egypt was concerned as the people of this land had also built columned temples, some of which appear to be forerunners of the later Greek, Doric architecture. However, it must also be on the cards that the actual details of the original Atlantian buildings had been entirely unknown to Plato and that when describing the island's chief city he rather appropriately added buildings which were Greek in style.

Indeed this is more than likely what had happened as there are a number of other aspects to the account which rather suggest that the author had indeed lacked such knowledge. One of these is the fact that the royal palace, which had been built immediately adjacent to the temple of Poseidon on the central hill, does not have any of its architectural features described in any way. On the contrary, all that we are told is that it was built according to a lavish design which was improved upon many times over by subsequent kings. What the building actually looked like or what it was made from is a complete unknown. But surely as the most important building of the city at least some description of it would have been warranted? Instead Plato proceeds to give us a fairly full description of the layout of Poseidon's temple standing beside it. Does this fact itself not suggest that the precise details of the Atlantian buildings were entirely unknown to Plato and that he merely added a Greek temple to the city for good measure?

However, things do not end there as there is further evidence of such 'Greek' additions.

Within the rings of land as well as upon the central island itself, we are told docks had been cut and where, according to Plato, fully equipped triremes had been moored. These latter ships can be considered as being entirely Greek in origin, having been introduced to this land sometime around 650 B.C. They are so called as they were propelled by three rows of oars on either side which were manned by a crew of up to two hundred. The advantage of such boats, despite being extremely labour intensive, was that they were not entirely dependant on the wind direction which made them ideal for ramming other vessels. Is it possible that such vessels had also been found among the people of Atlantis? It is true that the trireme's forerunner, the galley, which was powered by just a single row of oars and single sail, had been used extensively by the Mycenaeans and Minoans during the second millennium B.C. But nevertheless, Plato specifically says that the boats involved had been triremes. Again this must surely be put down to pure literary embellishment on Plato's part? Perhaps what he had meant to say was that the boats in question had been rowing boats that were also powered by sail, in other words, galleys, if indeed this had been the case?

Apart from doubts as to the authenticity of the details concerning the city and its contents, there are also questions as to the claims about the city's more ambitious of engineering constructions. The ditch, for example, which surrounded the entire plain, was said to have been some hundred feet in depth. Such was also the case for the canal which led from the city to the sea. Such a number of feet, apart from impressing upon us the incredible industriousness of the people of Atlantis, also leave us wondering what the precise purpose of such gargantuan projects had been? The canal, for example, from the city to the sea would have been deep enough to allow the passage both of a modern ocean liner and a nuclear submarine at the same time, let alone just a Greek trireme! The only credible suggestion which can be made for such an enormous depth to the ditches and canals surrounding the chief city of Atlantis, was to allow for the huge volume of water that flowed down from the surrounding mountains to the sea. Indeed we are told these mountains were the highest in the known world so presumably the rainfall they collected would have been high as well. But such a contrivance would surely have been fraught with hazards? The entire city would have been prone to flooding, strong currents and becoming silted up as any volume of water of that volume and power would be extremely difficult to manage in this respect.

A further point Plato's account is unclear on is the precise naming of the capital city already spoken of. Upon a cursory examination of the text one might be forgiven for assuming it had been the city that was called 'Atlantis', since a large part of the account covers the various details of its buildings and constructions. However, a more careful study reveals that it was actually the *island* that bore this name while the city had been apparently left unnamed by Plato. But why had this been the case—surely such an important city would have been given an appropriate name? It is tempting to assume that since the latter had been built within the kingdom of Atlas, who of course had ruled only one part of the island, about one tenth, that it had been named after the king himself. Instead, however, we are informed that it was actually the island that had been named after Atlas, being named rather aptly 'Atlantis'. But why had this been so if this particular king had only ruled *one tenth* of its land? Surely it would have been far more appropriate to have named the island after its founder, Poseidon? Indeed, for some authors, such appears to have been the case, as the island is sometimes described as being named 'Poseidonis'. Wouldn't it have been far more logical, therefore, to have named the city after its ruler, Atlas, and hence to have called it Atlantis while the larger island would be known as Poseidonis?

Indeed another peculiarity in Plato's account again would suggest that such a naming might have been the more appropriate is the fact that there are actually two islands that are actually spoken of rather than just the one. First, there is the island as whole which we have already described (and which we have also admitted could perhaps best be described as a continent being the size of 'Libya and Asia combined'); but then there is the central island which is surrounded by the concentric rings of water. It was upon this latter island that the city of Atlas had been built and one wonders whether this fact in itself offers a striking parallel to the main theme of the story that Atlantis had been an island on which King Atlas had founded his city? Had the island of Atlantis therefore actually been the hill surrounded by the concentric rings of water and on which the capital city was located? Of course, this would necessitate an alternative name for the larger continent, and such a name has already been suggested in the form of Poseidonis.

And what of the destruction of Atlantis? If the devastation had only affected the smaller island and its accompanying city, then it must have been the case that the larger continent could have remained intact? As has already been mentioned, the smaller island was also the location for hot springs which had caused us to speculate that perhaps its origins had been volcanic. Was this fact itself the cause of the localised devastation? Since the island in question is described as a hill, we can only assume that it had perhaps also been an active volcano? However, Plato informs us that the hill was only small in size which is unusual for a volcano, which more often takes the form of a mountain. Had it been the case that Plato in his account of the story had reduced the size of the hill in favour of the island, which he had then claimed had been called Atlantis and had disappear without a trace? It seems probable that such could have been the case as in recorded history there are far more examples of mountains that have simply exploded leaving few remains than we have of islands or even entire continents that have just disappeared into the sea.

So if the hill upon the island-continent had been an active volcano, then why had the inhabitants taken the obvious risk of building a city within its vicinity, or even upon its slopes? It is quite possible that the people concerned were entirely unaware that the mountain had been a volcano as it was more than likely in a state of dormancy at the time. Indeed there are many examples from around the world of settlements that have sprung up within a close proximity to such mountains. At certain points in time some of these volcanoes inevitably became active again, erupting with devastating consequences. Had this been the fate that was suffered by the inhabitants of Atlantis?

One final point worthy of discussion concerns the various attributes of the island's founder, Poseidon. In Greek mythology not only is he the lord of all the seas but he is also known as the 'earth-shaker'. According to story he is armed with a trident and it is with this that he is able to shatter rocks, causing them to fall into the sea. As a result of this it could be considered as rather appropriate that Poseidon should have been associated with such an island-continent after it had suffered such a fate. At the very end of Plato's account of the story he describes Zeus as gatherings the gods together to pronounce judgement upon the islanders, but what precisely happens next is a mystery as Plato had left the account unfinished. It is obvious that the island is subsequently destroyed by some form of earthquake so would it not have been appropriate if it had been Poseidon himself who had to carry out this awesome destruction? If Plato had had the opportunity to finish his account, then perhaps he would have described Poseidon as rising from the waters and crashing his trident upon the sides of the mountains?

However, whether the island had been destroyed by a devastating earthquake or by a volcanic eruption, the point still remains that the story most likely refers to some ancient catastrophe in which a city that was comparatively advanced for its day was suddenly destroyed without warning.

2

Diodorus Siculus: Amazons and Atlantians

Based in Sicily in the first century B.C., Diodorus Siculus was the author of a history based upon a whole series of myths and legends that he had gathered from all around the ancient world. These he had compiled rather uncritically but it is by virtue of this that we are so much the richer in such material. Of course, not all of Diodorus' work has survived, but what we do have gives us a valuable insight into a rich prehistory that would otherwise have been long forgotten. Indeed, one group of people the author speaks of in Book III is the Atlantians. However it is apparent that Diodorus' account of the people is very different in character to that given by Plato. Nevertheless, there are still a number of key similarities which will be the subject of much discussion in this chapter.

According to Diodorus' account, the Atlantians had been a race who had dwelt in a fertile land lying towards the larger ocean of the world. They apparently possessed a number of myths which, so he claimed, did not differ greatly from those of the Greeks. They maintained that their first king had been Uranus himself who had gathered together all the people of the region and housed them within a single city that he surrounded with a wall. It was also Uranus who had taught his people the art of civilisation and who had given them their first laws. Having established his city, the king then commenced to conquer the lands lying immediately to the west and to the north. Uranus had also, so it was claimed, been skilful in the art of astronomy and foretold many future events.

The story goes that Uranus fathered forty-five sons, eighteen of whom were by Titea, who by virtue of this became known as Titans. As a result of Titea's benevolence towards her people she was named Gaia, after the Earth. However, Uranus also sired daughters, the eldest of whom were Basilea and Rhea. Being the eldest, Basilea assisted in the raising of her younger brothers until she eventually married one of her siblings, Hyperion. The two bore the children Helius and Selene who were both of great beauty. However, the brothers of the two were jealous and, fearing they would take the crown for themselves, murdered Hyperion, throwing his son into the river Epidanus. When Selene heard of this she was inconsolable and took her own life. However, Basilea received a vision in which each of her offspring became immortals, Helius the sun and Selene the moon, and this was how the two were subsequently remembered.

Some time after this Uranus decided to divide his kingdom equally between his sons, the most notable of whom were Atlas and Cronus. The lands Atlas received lay towards the greater ocean and the name consequently given to his people was the Atlantians. Also named after the king was the largest mountain of the region being called Mount Atlas. It was also said that the science of astrology had been discovered here by virtue of the fact that Atlas had borne the entire heavens upon his shoulders. King Atlas fathered a number of sons, the most notable of whom was Hesperus. The latter, however, did not live to old age as he was swept away one day by strong winds from the top of Mount Atlas, having attempted to ascend its summit.

Atlas also fathered seven daughters, the Atlantides, who, apart from their fairness, were also considered as the progenitors of man. It was they who reared the many heroes who would later become famous for their epic exploits. With their passing, the sisters were placed in the sky forever in the form of the constellation of seven stars known today as the Pleiades.

Having sufficiently covered the myths and legends of this people, Diodorus then returns to the subject of the Atlantians themselves specifically in connection with the Amazons, the fearful all-women tribe with whom they did battle. The latter were said to have dwelt upon an island in the west known as Hespera which had been situated in the middle of a large lake, Tritonis. Again the lake lay towards the larger ocean that surrounded the entire world and was fed by the river Triton. Ethiopia was not that far from here and neither was the large mountain adjacent to the shore called Atlas. The island was large in size and supported many varied herds and fruit-bearing trees. However at this particular time cereal was still not grown.

The Amazons, being the foremost inhabitants of the island on which they lived in Lake Tritonis, set out to conquer each of the cities found upon it. The city that they called Mena however they left untouched as it was considered as sacred. It was inhabited by Ethiopian Ichthyophages and the entire area surrounding it was prone to volcanic eruptions, though it was also extremely rich in precious stone. After their subsequent victories the Amazons founded a vast city called Cherronesus after its shape, as it was built along the length of a ridge that jutted out into the lake.

Having thus established their prowess in battle, the Amazons then set out to conquer other parts of the world under the leadership of their queen Myrina. The first people they encountered, of course, were the Atlantians who apparently were the most civilised race of the region. The latter had also built large cities and it was said that the birthplace of the immortals themselves was to be found in their lands. Myrina gathered together an army consisting of 30,000 infantry and some 3,000 cavalry. As armour they wore snakeskin as apparently in this part of the land there were many of these creatures. Her warriors were much skilled in the use of the bow as indeed they were with both the sword and the spear.

The first city of the Atlantians that they came across was Cerna. With brave determination the Amazons succeeded in broaching its walls and once inside they then savaged the population so as to deliberately cause panic among its neighbours. When their fellow Atlantians had heard the news of the latter's fall they submitted themselves entirely to the Amazon queen. In memory of her victory, Myrina constructed a new city upon the ruins of the old, naming it after herself. Now allied with the Amazons, the Atlantians suggested that they first raid their most feared and hated enemy, the Gorgons. When the two opposing armies had lined up, a great battle was fought in which the Amazon warriors again prevailed. The surviving Gorgons then fled to the wilds, closely pursued by the warrior queen Myrina. She ordered the ground around them to be set ablaze in a final attempt to destroy this race once and for all, though with a greater or lesser degree of success.

The following night when Myrina's people were celebrating their success, their captives all of a sudden turned upon their Amazon guards and succeeded in killing a great number of them before finally falling themselves. In honour of her fallen warriors, Myrina built three great pyres, piling earth on top of them to create what are still known today as the "Amazon Mounds".

However, the Gorgons soon regained their original strength and it took the hero Perseus to finally defeat them along with their evil queen Medusa. Later Heracles was finally to destroy the last of them along with the Amazons themselves while making his visit to Libya to set up his famous pillars. Also around this time it is said that an earthquake caused the entire lake called Tritonis to suddenly disappear and the surrounding land was also torn open.

Myrina, however, continued her onward march through Libya before entering Egypt where she became friendly with the king of Egypt, Horus. She then commenced a battle with the Arabians and the Syrians, conquering many lands in the process. After this she proceeded to defeat the people of the Taurus and then entered Greater Phrygia where she made her way to the Mediterranean. Following the coast, Myrina got as far as the Caicus River where she founded a number of cities that she named after herself and each of her commanders.

Myrina had also conquered much territory further inland in addition to a number of islands which included Lesbos where she founded the city of Mitylena, named after her sister. During her campaign against these latter islands, however, she was caught in a ferocious storm. After asking for the protection of her patron deity she was carried to the safety of an uninhabited island which was subsequently named "Samothrace", or 'sacred isle'.

Around this time Mopsus, a Thracian, led an army against the Amazons allied with Sipylus, a Scythian. A mighty battle took place as a result of which Myrina and most of her army were slain. After an interval of some years and several further defeats, the Amazons finally withdrew back to Africa.

So concludes Diodorus' account of the Amazons and the Atlantians as delivered in Book III of his World History. The first thing that immediately strikes us about the story is that it differs from Plato in the chief fact that it is actually the Amazons rather than the Atlantians who do battle with the Greeks. Myrina, their queen, first gains control of a large part of Africa before conquering parts of Asia Minor previously held by the Greeks. In Plato's account, however, it is actually the Atlantians who gain control of large parts of Libya and the northern coast of the Mediterranean before finally being repulsed. The latter being said to have issued from beyond the Pillars of Heracles from an island in the Atlantic they inhabited immediately adjacent to the straits of Gibraltar rather than from Africa itself.

But which of the two accounts was actually the correct one in this respect? Was it the Atlantians or the Amazons against whom the Greeks had so bitterly fought? As far as the classical authors in general are concerned, the consensus of opinion appears to be that it was actually the Amazons who had challenged the might of the Greeks many centuries before in Asia Minor. Indeed in ancient Greece itself there were numerous commemorations of these very battles and their mythology is richly infused with such stories of these all-female war-riors, many of whom are remembered by name. So why such a glaring difference? It has already been made apparent that Plato had been tell-ing a bit of a story when he emphasised quite how advanced the Atlan-tians had been. Partly this was to demonstrate the point that a perfect society was, at least in theory, indeed possible. But it could be argued that Plato hadn't been that far wrong when stating the extent of their influence, only he had omitted to inform us of the important point that the Atlantians had actually first joined forces with the Amazons before they did this.

But if this is how things had happened, then what of the island beyond the Pillars of Heracles? Diodorus also mentions these pillars, but it appears that Heracles himself only sets them up after having first defeated the last of the Amazon tribe in Libya. The very fact that the land in question lay beyond these 'pillars' does not necessarily preclude the possibility that they lay directly to their south for example. Could Plato have been equally inaccurate on this point as well? Of course, this would have entailed the Atlantians, like the Amazons, having dwelt within the lands of Libya as was indeed the case stated by Diodorus. As a result of this it would appear that the island beyond the Pillars of Heracles spoken of by Plato could actually have been the land mass which lay directly to their south, or in other words the continent of Africa.

But was there any real historical substance to the story of the Ama-zons anyway? Surely the whole thing is just pure fable? In some respects at least this would appear to be the case as some of the details of the tribe given by Diodorus in Book II of his histories are somewhat larger than life. Indeed most ancient historians would feel inclined to class the entire story of the Amazons as pure myth, but who is to say that the story does not at least have some basis in that it referred to a very ancient outpouring of peoples from the continent of Africa and that this outpouring was eventually held in check by the Greeks them-selves?

However, putting this question aside, here is the description of the tribe as given by Diodorus. Apparently their chief custom for which they gained their fame was that all their rulers were female and it was also the latter sex who were responsible for any acts of valour on the battlefield. Men, it would appear, very much took second place and were assigned the more menial tasks that the women would otherwise have performed. To maintain this status quo the Amazons were in the habit of practising the rather cruel custom of maiming all the male infants by crippling their arms and legs. However, the female offspring of this tribe did not escape such cruel treatment either, as each suffered injury of having their right breast removed. But apparently there was also some reason in this in that this better equipped them for drawing the bow. Indeed it was for this reason that the tribe was given its name, which means literally 'without a breast'. All the women were trained from an early age in the art of war and the foremost among them, both in skill and physical strength, was chosen as queen.

An interesting detail Diodorus gives to us in his account is the fact that he mentions that their queen, Myrina, entered into friendly relations with the king of Egypt, Horus. Of course the latter, as anyone with the slightest knowledge of Egyptian mythology will tell you, had been the son of Osiris, the legendary first king and founder of Egypt. The myth goes that the latter had been killed by his evil brother Seth and as a consequence was made first lord of the underworld. His son Horus meanwhile took over as earthly ruler. Since it is apparent that both these figures are largely mythological in nature and were perhaps created in order to explain the origins of the royal line in Egypt, wouldn't we be justified in placing these events in the pre-dynastic era of ancient Egypt, that is, prior to 3,000 B.C.? Whether or not Osiris and Horus are in any way based upon real historical, ancestor figures, is not necessarily the point; what matters is that the events in question took place shortly before the founding of pharaonic Egypt.

However Diodorus' account also reveals certain other historical facts which we know must be open to question. For example he mentions that the Amazon warriors were experts on horseback and had mastered the technique of firing their arrows directly behind them whilst fleeing the enemy. Indeed, the use of cavalry, so he tells us, was their favoured method in war. Indeed in their battles with the Atlantians they had used three thousand of such warriors accompanied by thirty thousand foot. But if the use of the horse had indeed been their favoured method, then surely these figures are the wrong way around; surely it should have been thirty thousand cavalry accompanied by three thousand foot? However a far more important question is where exactly had the Amazons obtained all their horses from in the first place?

The horse that we are all so familiar with is certainly not native to Africa but is usually imported into the continent via the Near East. The Egyptians had made extensive use of the horse, commencing from the 17th century B.C., having imported it along with the chariot—but before this the animal had not been known in the continent. Assuming that the battles between the Amazons and the Atlantians had taken place sometime prior to 3,000 B.C., that is, before pharaonic Egypt had come to be, then the tribe could not therefore have had access to such animals and hence could not have had a cavalry as such. The only nearest equivalents indigenous to Africa are, of course, the wild ass and the zebra, which are certainly fairly ill equipped for riding on in battle. Perhaps it is possible to imagine these women for a moment, being lighter in build and with appropriate training, riding on the backs of zebras, a fact which may have given them a slight advantage over their nearest rivals? But it is still doubtful whether these creatures would have been either strong or fast enough during the hectic din of battle to have carried such a burden.

Another detail of the account which must also be open to question is the precise state of advancement of the Amazon tribe. Diodorus states that on the island where they had lived there were many trees bearing fruit as well as herds from which they obtained their sustenance. However he also emphasises the point that the cultivation of wheat had still as yet not been discovered. This would imply that the

Amazons were hunter gatherers, as no mention is made of the cultivation of the fruit trees on the island or of their rearing of the herds mentioned. Indeed one can only assume the latter were wild. But if the Amazons had lived in such a primitive state upon this island, then the question has to be asked how did they come to be so well armed? Diodorus states that not only had they discovered the bow and arrow but they had also developed the spear and the sword. The latter weapon especially must surely imply that the knowledge of metal working was present among them, clearly implying that they were of at least some state of advancement. Indeed, perhaps they had already entered the Bronze Age, like their near neighbours, the Atlantians may well already have done if what Plato tells us about them was true. However, one might have expected that such advances in the working of metal would have at least been accompanied by similar advances in farming? Indeed, how were the men of the tribe to occupy themselves all day other than with the picking of fruit and hunting down of the herds? In spite of this however, it is still possible that the Amazons were significantly less advanced than the Atlantians were who, as Diodorus informs us, were the most highly advanced people of the region.

Having already established the fact that it was actually the Amazons rather than the Atlantians who, in legend at least, invaded much of North Africa and challenged the might of the Greeks in Asia Minor, there is a further point of difference between the stories told by Diodorus and Plato. Whereas in the latter account it was the Atlantians who had owned the island surrounded by water, in the former it was the Amazons. It had been this tribe who had dwelt upon the island known as Hespera in the middle of the large lake Triton. Also, there appears to have been several cities upon this island, one of which was the subject of volcanic eruptions. The latter had been owned by Ethiopian Ichthyophages, who were so named as a result of the manner in which they gained their sustenance. Had this city, which was named Mena, been the same as that described by Plato which had been built upon the hill containing the hot and cold springs? Like Mena, this city had also possessed some sacred, ceremonial significance, as it was the site of a very important shrine.

Another striking similarity between the two accounts which again might indicate that Mena had been the same city as that described by Plato, was the fact that as a result of the volcanic activity found upon it, it was particularly rich in precious stone. Diodorus states that it was particularly rich in three of these, sardion, anthrax and smaragdos. These stones are respectively orange, deep red, and green. Interestingly enough the stone described by Plato which was used in much of the construction work on Atlantis, also came in three different colours, these being white, black and yellow. If the city of Mena had also been rich is such coloured stone, then presumably it would most likely have been used, if not for constructional purposes, then at least for decoration.

Diodorus also tells us that it is volcanic activity, or rather more specifically seismic activity in general, that leads to the eventual destruction of the island called Hespera. However there is one important twist to this; rather than the entire island itself, or even the continental land mass sinking into the sea as Plato has it, it is actually the lake that disappears leaving the island high and dry. Of course, if the water itself surrounding the island were to completely vanish, it would mean that the island would no longer be an island and many of its buildings and defences would be rendered completely useless. Cherronesus, the chief city of the Amazons, which had been built along the length of a natural prominence in the lake, would have been left rather exposed and its harbours would have been made completely redundant. Also, the Ethiopian Ichthyophages that dwelt in the city of Mena, would have been left without their chief source of food. So even though these two cities were not directly destroyed in the seismic events spoken of, the resultant loss of the lake could well have led to their eventual abandon.

We can only speculate as to what the wider impact of these events had been? Diodorus, for example, states that it was almost as if the Earth itself had been torn apart in this region, suggesting that the earthquake in question had been quite devastating. Certainly for the ground to have opened, allowing water on its surface to seep through, suggests a substantial shift in the Earth's crust. Accompanying phenomena would inevitably have included landslides and collapsed buildings. However, a further phenomena that can occur as the result of an earthquake is the altering of river courses. Diodorus tells us that the lake in question had been fed by a river—so had this river altered its course due to the effects of the earthquake? If it had, then it is possible that the lake had simply dried up as a result of this. Indeed, all we are told by Diodorus is that the lake simply disappeared and he does not specify exactly how and over what period of time we are speaking of. Possibly the lake had indeed vanished as a direct result of the seismic activity, but the event in question had been far from sudden and the lake dried gradually as a result of the loss of its supply of water.

It is also far from clear whether it was this event which had ultimately led to the downfall of the Amazons and the Atlantians or whether such had occurred as a direct result of the intervention of other tribes or peoples. For example Diodorus says that both the Amazons and their closest rivals, the Gorgons, had been entirely defeated by Heracles when he had set his pillars up in Libya. But the implication still remains that the earthquake had played an important part for immediately after relating the event he speaks of the lake's disappearance. In fact, such a scenario seems likely, for if one considers the rivalry that had existed between the tribes of this region, such an event which particularly weakened the dominant tribe could well have led to their eventual defeat at the hands of their rivals. Such a juxtaposition of events is also found in Plato, as the Greeks, having defeated the Atlantians who had invaded through Asia Minor, then followed their foe to their island habitation where they were then the witnesses of a widespread destruction.

Another curious aspect of Diodorus' account is the fact that the rival tribes of the Amazons and the Atlantians occupy two quite distinct and yet equally dramatic landscapes. The Amazons, for example, occupy the island Hespera which lies in a lake of largish proportions, while the Atlantians, who are not that far away, dwell within the close proximity of a tall mountain called Atlas. We know that the latter must have been large in size as it was named after the Titan Atlas who supported the entire heavens upon his shoulders. It is possible, therefore, that on most days its summit reached high into the clouds such that it appeared to be supporting the entire sky. It is also likely that the mountain was the object of much veneration, as the immortals were considered to have been born at this place. Again according to Diodorus, this mountain lay towards the sea and was surrounded by a rich fertile plain. In this respect we are reminded of Plato's hill in the middle of the rectangular plain on which Atlantis was built and which was also situated facing the sea.

Within a close proximity to this mountain called Atlas, the first king of the Atlantians, Uranus, had constructed a walled city. He taught its inhabitants the art of cultivation and he was also their first lawgiver. Perhaps this had been the same as the city called Cerna which Diodorus describes as the Atlantian city which was razed to the ground by the Amazons and which was also surrounded by a wall? Perhaps as a result of its being the chief city of the Atlantians, its capture had struck such terror into its immediate neighbours? Uranus having added many lands to those he already owned, decided to divide his kingdom equally between his sons. Foremost among these had been Atlas who had received the allotment containing the mountain and its city. In this respect Diodorus' account is also remarkably similar to that of Plato's where Atlas, as one of the kings of Atlantis, receives the allotment containing the hill on which he builds his city.

Another interesting aspect of the story worth reflecting upon is the precise naming of the island in Lake Triton, Hespera. Of course, the island had been called this as it had lain in the west, the name literally meaning towards the west or the evening. However, the lake that it was found in was said to have been situated towards Ethiopia which is actually in the east. Perhaps the island had instead been named Hespera by virtue of the fact that it had been located to the west of Mount Atlas rather than being situated on the western side of the continent in question? In fact, if this had been the situation, then such would have been a completely logical manner of assigning names as the two features, which lay side by side, mountain and lake, would have been intimately interlinked in the minds of the ancient geographers. The largest mountain in the area, being in possession of King Atlas, was consequently named after him, while the island in the lake to the west of it was called Hespera, designating its geographical position in relation to the former.

It is also apparent that for the lake to have warranted such an important record being made of it, alongside a mountain which is described as having been the tallest in the entire region, it must have been of some significant dimensions itself. Certainly, Diodorus states that the island situated within it was generously proportioned, so it only follows that the lake was also of some size itself. Indeed it would appear that the island was large enough to accommodate quite a number of cities inhabited by distinctly separate peoples prior to the Amazon conquest of them. But even though there is little doubt as to the fact that the lake had covered a comparatively large area, there is some question as to its average depth since some translators have described it as more of a marsh as such rather than a lake. Across the globe there are many examples of marshes fed by rivers covering quite large areas of land and when these are encountered they can prove exceptionally difficult to cross. Indeed, if Tritonis had been a marsh rather than a lake, the Amazons must have encountered the same problem, for how could they have left the confines of their island without sinking in its mires? When the water levels were low, vast stretches of mud would have appeared which would have been completely impassable and a bridge or causeway would have been necessary. However, assuming that Lake Tritonis had been of quite large dimensions, it is obvious that a bridge would have been necessary which itself would have needed to have been of a generous length to have spanned the mud flats. And we can only imagine the hazards presented in the construction of such a feature. Indeed, if Tritonis had been such a boggy, inhospitable expanse of mud, then how could the Ethiopian Ichthyophages have obtained their livelihood from it in the form of fishing?

It seems probable, therefore, that the lake must have had at least some depth to it. Indeed, the fact that the Amazonian city of Cherronesus had been built along the length of a ridge that jutted into it suggests some variation of high and low ground. This variation would suggest water accumulating at the bottom of hollows forming a lake rather than the flat expanse of a marsh. Indeed further doubt is cast upon the accuracy of describing Tritonis as a marsh as volcanic activity had been present on Hespera, which suggests that the landscape was undergoing a gradual process of change anyway, a process that would eventually lead to the disappearance of Tritonis and its island. And again the very fact that Diodorus states that the watery expanse of Tritonis had entirely disappeared from view in a relatively short space of time, again suggests that it must have contained quite some water for it to have been so apparently visible in the first place.

An interesting detail in the history of the Amazons is the fact that their leadership throughout almost all of their conquests was filled by just the one individual, their queen Myrina. It was the latter who had led her armies against the rival cities on the island of Hespera, conquering each of them in turn; and it was she who had led the Amazons to victory against the Atlantians. Having conquered their main rivals, the Gorgons, Myrina also entered other parts of Libya and, after having made a treaty with the king of Egypt, then marched into Asia Minor. Here she proved a rival to the Greeks themselves, founding many cities. Having won all of these victories, Myrina was finally defeated by the Greek leader Mopsus. However, this did not prove to be the final end of the Amazons whose continued presence was felt in this land.

After Myrina a number of successive queens are spoken of but by this time the strength of the Amazon armies was already beginning to dwindle. These rulers were especially present around the region of the

Thermodon river on the Pontus in Asia Minor. It was here at Themiscyra, that their royal palace was built. When Heracles had been set his task of procuring the girdle of the Amazon queen Hippolyta, he brought his armies to Themiscyra, having first sailed along the Thermodon river. Having been defeated by Heracles, the Amazon army then joined forces with the Scythians. The next hero Theseus however put a stop to the advance of this combined army and those that had the chance fled to Scythia.

Penthesileia, who had originally fled her country as the result of a crime she had committed, rejoined the remaining members of her tribe in Asia Minor, making herself their queen. She joined forces with the Trojans during their war against the Greeks but her efforts were to no avail. According to the story, Penthesileia was slain by the hero Achilles. After this the remaining Amazons either dispersed or returned to Libya.

This is the sum of what Diodorus tells us about the Amazons and their closest rivals, the Atlantians, who they defeated in battle. However, the story does not quite end here as elsewhere in Greek literature there is further reference to Mount Atlas and Lake Triton.

3

In Greek Myth and Legend

Among the many myths and legends present among those of the ancient Greeks, Mount Atlas and the island of Hespera specifically have their place where they are the site of further heroic endeavours. Had such a land ever existed at the very periphery of the known world, it would have been an ideal location for any story told with the intention of creating a sense of wonder in its audience. Possibly based upon geographical and historical fact, all that was then required was that the land in question be appropriately kitted out with supernatural beings and beasts for the heroes to do battle with. Indeed, Diodorus Siculus has already mentioned that this region had been visited by the heroes Perseus and Heracles. Whether these visits refer to actual historical events or are purely fictitious creations, is, of course, entirely open to debate. In the meantime all we can do is relate these stories as they were given by the Greeks themselves.

The story of the various exploits of the hero Perseus is revealed to us in both a colourful and a lyrical manner by the poet Ovid. Although based in Rome, the author still managed to capture the very essence of the Greek story. In order to save his mother from the cruelty of Polydectes, the tyrannical ruler of the island of Seriphos, Perseus set himself the task of bringing back the head of Medusa, the most feared of the three Gorgons. To do this necessitated travelling to faraway lands where he encountered the direst of perils.

With the aid of his winged sandals given to him by Mercury, Perseus eventually arrived at the furthest horizon where Mount Atlas towered above the shore of the world's larger ocean. Here, at the base of the mountain, within a cave, the two daughters of Phorcys dwelt. These two wretches shared between them a single eye which they passed between themselves to view the world. When Perseus had located the cave he used all his stealth to steal the eye as they were passing it from one to the other. As a price for its return Perseus demanded that they tell him the way to the abode of Medusa, the Gorgon.

Having gleaned the desired information, the hero travelled across rugged and inhospitable terrain to arrive at his intended destination. For some distance it became apparent that he was getting closer to his quarry as along the way he encountered the frozen images of men and creatures who had been turned to stone. Forewarned of the danger of catching Medusa's gaze square on, he proceeded while looking at the reflection in his shield. However Perseus must have had the luck of the immortals on his side as when he arrived at her lair, Medusa was sleeping. Without making a sound, Perseus took his sword and lopped off her head with one blow. From the blood which issued from the gapping wound, a winged horse sprouted forth called Pegasus.

Mounting his new found steed, Perseus soared high into the air, making rapid headway above the lands of Libya. While carrying the head of Medusa at his side, some of its blood fell to the ground causing hordes of snakes to rise up. Apparently it is for this reason that the land to this day is so full of such creatures.

As the towering heights of Mount Atlas loomed towards them, Pegasus swooped down to alight on its lower slopes. Here luscious fields were found which supplied rich grazing for countless herds. Also not far from here was an orchard in which golden apples grew. Perseus, not forgetting he was a guest, respectfully asked Atlas if he could be allowed a moment's rest at this spot. The Titan, however, had not forgotten the prediction that one day a foreigner would arrive at his land and rob him of his golden fruit. Indeed, to prevent such an eventuality, Atlas had surrounded his orchard with a tall wall and set a fearsome looking serpent to guard it. Atlas rather sternly replied to Perseus that perhaps he ought to be on his way. When Perseus proved rather unobliging, Atlas began to grumble. Being no match for the Titan, Perseus had another course of action at hand and grabbing the Gorgon's head, held it up before the giant. The story according to Ovid goes that Atlas immediately began to turn to stone to the extent that his shoulders, which had previously supported the sky, became an awesome mountain summit. Perseus, not wishing to take on the dreadful serpent guarding the apples, quickly went on his way as he had other duties to perform in a land not far from here.

Thus concludes the story of the obtaining of the Gorgon's head by the hero Perseus. Among the ancient Greeks the various themes of this story had always had a great appeal and they appear with striking regularity very early on in their art. The winged Pegasus and the Gorgon's head, for example, were used as motifs as early as the 7th century B.C.—so it seems that the myth itself had quite ancient origins even before its retelling by Ovid.

As with Diodorus, so it is also quite apparently the case with Ovid, that the Gorgons dwelt in a land that was not that far from the base of a large mountain called Atlas. It would have been logical enough for Perseus to have first visited the mountain in order to obtain knowledge of their precise whereabouts if he already knew that they dwelt within its close proximity. Indeed, his journey from the cave to Medusa's lair also suggests that, even though they did not inhabit the territory immediately surrounding Atlas itself, it was at least in a land that was not far from it.

One immediate point of difference, however, between Ovid and Diodorus, is the actual number of Gorgons involved. In the former and also elsewhere in classical literature, the legendary Medusa has two sisters, Sthenno and Euryale, who are in many ways equally terrifying. However, Diodorus without doubt has the Gorgons as mortal stock who, like the Amazons, are represented in the more plural form as a tribe of women. Indeed he tells us that they were the sworn rivals of the Amazons until the latter finally got the better of them. So why the difference? The immediate answer to this must lie in the distinction between legend and myth. On the one hand there is an account based upon actual historical happenings, although a rather vague one, involving a tribe of fearsome women, and on the other there is a story of a hero battling against overwhelming odds with supernatural creatures. If Ovid and Diodorus are compared side by side it is not too difficult to see how history became legend and then finally transformed itself into myth in the shape of the story of Perseus's quest to bring back the head of Medusa.

It would also appear to be the case that the number three was of symbolic significance as this number is often used by story tellers to denote plurality. Hence, rather than being just a single clutch of sisters, the Gorgons could actually have represented an entire race. Also, it was probably as a result of their bravery in battle and their fearsome reputation, that they were given their dreadful, unladylike looks.

But what of the horde of snakes that crowned the head of Medusa? Did these also possess symbolic value or were they a reference to something else entirely? It is tempting to hold the possibility that this figure, as the leader of the Gorgons or even their queen, as her name Medusa would appear to reveal, had been in the habit of tying live snakes in her hair so as to appear all the more fearsome on the battlefield. Assuming that the snakes she had chosen for this purpose had not been poisonous, the effect could have been quite stunning. Indeed perhaps it had not just been Medusa who had adorned herself in this way but all of the tribe of Gorgons. This fact alone could have so terrified their enemies to the extent that the sight of them charging into battle had almost frozen them to the spot. Such an explanation of the myth is indeed tempting especially when it is considered that Diodorus himself informs us that the Amazon tribe were in the habit of wearing snakeskin armour due to the frequency with which this creature occurred in the region. If the Amazons had been in the habit of using snakeskin as armour, perhaps the Gorgans had been in the habit of using it as a type of weapon?

In Diodorus, Medusa is indeed the queen of the Gorgon tribe and he has Perseus travelling into Libya to take on the might of the tribe who eventually succeeds in defeating them. Of course, having won such a decisive victory, it would only have been appropriate to have taken the queen's head as trophy surely? Perhaps the hero Perseus, under the guidance of king Polydectes, had then brought the head back home with him in order to show it to his patron? Having taken the head from its place of containment, having been appropriately preserved for the journey, perhaps it had also been the case that snakes had still adorned its hair?

The next Greek myth which makes mention of Mount Atlas and the Hesperides, is that concerning Heracles and his labours. This latter figure, who had apparently visited this region some time after Perseus had completed his task, had also been responsible for defeating the Amazon tribe as well as the last remnants of the Gorgons. The story is related by Diodorus in Book IV of his Histories. Apparently the hero was set twelve almost impossible labours by King Eurystheus on condition that if he completed them he would be granted the gift of immortality. Among these labours was the slaying of various mythical creatures and the bringing back of the girdle of the Amazon Hippolyta. The last labour he was required to perform was the retrieval of the golden apples from the garden of the Hesperides. In order to do this, he had first to journey to Libya where the garden was located.

According to the story, the land in question was called Hesperitis and in it two brothers dwelt, Hesperus and Atlas. The former had sired a daughter called Hespris whom he had given in marriage to Atlas. The couple had then produced seven delightful young daughters known as the Atlantides, but also sometimes the Hesperides. It was the latter whose role it was to tend to the garden containing the golden fruit which in turn was guarded by a ferocious serpent.

Apparently however, there was some dispute as to whether the 'fruit' concerned were not actually sheep, as the Greek word used ('melon') can mean either. Indeed, it was known that the land had been particularly prosperous in these herds and due to their fine quality it was suggested that they had perhaps been described as 'golden' as a consequence. However, it was also a possibility that their wool had possessed a pronounced yellow colouration to it which would also have warranted the same description. Some indeed have even claimed, though it must be added rather humorously, that the serpent guarding them, 'Dracon', had actually been the name of a shepherd who was given this appellation as a result of the rather eager manner in which he guarded his flock. Whatever the case, Heracles had to slay this guardian before he could make off with his precious quarry.

Before undertaking this task, Heracles, being the undeniable hero that he was, first undertook another mission to rectify a wrong that had been committed. The king of Egypt, Busiris, had recently kidnapped the Atlantides as a result of the fact that he had coveted the chastity of these fair maidens. In order to retrieve them, Heracles first slew the wrestler Antaeus in Libya and then travelled onwards to Egypt, making sure that Busiris himself suffered the same fate. Sailing back along the Nile, he also defeated the Ethiopian king Emathion. Heracles then encountered the pirates who had been responsible for the kidnapping, moored upon a sandy shore and defeated each of them one by one. After this he took the girls home again, returning them to their father. Atlas, as a result of his gratitude to Heracles, assisted him in his primary deed of retrieving the golden apples as well as tutoring him in the art of astrology. Indeed, it is said that for this last reason Heracles is considered to have shouldered the heavens when he received this knowledge.

Diodorus does not go into any further detail than this, and would appear that the main obstacle in the performance of Heracles' last deed was the return of the Atlantides rather than the slaying of the dragon and retrieving the golden apples. As in Ovid's story of Perseus, it is Atlas who is the rightful owner of the garden—his seven daughters, the Atlantides, also sometimes known as the Hesperides after their mother, being given the responsibility of tending to the garden. However,

Diodorus also states that the land Hesperitis was actually owned by two bothers, Atlas and Hesperus. Indeed, it was the daughter of the latter whom Atlas had married and who bore his seven daughters, the Hesperides. In this respect the account is a direct parallel of his first in which two distinct kingdoms are centred around the island of Hespera and Mount Atlas. The king of each, presuming the land had been named after them, would of course have been Hesperus and Atlas. At least this is one explanation, but in point of fact the ruler of the former, according to Diodorus' first account, had actually been an Amazon queen, Myrina. However, this does not mean to say that a king called Hesperus had not previously existed on the island immediately prior to its being conquered by the Amazons who indeed were later to conquer the Atlantians themselves.

In fact king Hesperus is indeed mentioned in Diodorus' first account where it is related that he had attempted to ascend Mount Atlas only to be swept away by strong winds. In this instance, however, Hesperus is described as having been the son of Atlas rather than his brother, but as a king then presumably he would have ruled over lands that were quite separate from those of Atlas. Had these lands also been those immediately surrounding Lake Tritonis and its island Hespera? If such an arrangement had occurred, then it's quite possible that it referred to a time immediately prior to the arrival of the Amazons on the scene. In any case, it is apparent that the island had been named after its earlier king, Hesperus, rather than Myrina who was later to be its queen.

It is quite apparent from Diodorus' first account that the island in Lake Tritonis was particularly rich in fruit trees as well as herds that also roamed upon it. So had it perhaps been the case that the island in Lake Tritonis was the garden spoken of containing the trees which bore the golden fruit? Certainly, the name is almost the same, the garden of the Hesperides, and it again was only a short stop from the slopes of Mount Atlas. So had the garden actually been an island? The very fact that it was described as a garden does indeed imply that it was enclosed in some way, but had this means of enclosure been entirely natural rather than man-made? Upon an island walls for defensive purposes are not as vitally necessary as they are elsewhere, as the water forms a natural barrier against unwanted persons straying onto one's land. Ovid quite clearly states that the garden had been protected by a tall wall, but this still does not preclude the possibility that the wall had been present upon an island. Indeed it is quite possible for a garden to be present upon an island even though the author in question at that particular point does not mention this fact. So was this island garden therefore none other than Hespera which had been located within Lake Tritonis?

In Diodorus' first account, where the island of Hespera and Mount Atlas are quite clearly distinctly different territories, it was the chief city of the Atlantians not far from the foot of the Mount Atlas which had been surrounded by a wall. Having been founded by King Uranus, the purpose of the wall was to protect the inhabitants within rather than for the guarding of any fruit trees. It is true, of course, that the cultivation of fruit had been important to this people, this art having been taught to them by Uranus himself; but the latter had very much been for purpose of providing food rather than for the raising of any crop of peculiar significance. It could be suggested therefore that perhaps it had been this city, built not that far from the base of Mount Atlas, that Ovid had been thinking of when he stated that a large wall had been built around the garden so as to protect it and he had merely transferred this to the Island of Hespera.

While performing his last labour, Diodorus tells us that Heracles bore the weight of the sky upon his shoulders, at least for a short time. In alternative accounts, Heracles does this so that Atlas can obtain the apples on his behalf, but upon his return the Titan refuses to take up the burden once more. With shrewd cunning, however, Heracles manages to trick the Titan into resuming his duty, and while he does this he quickly makes his getaway. However Diodorus also informs us that it was not so much the weight of the sky that had been passed between their shoulders as the science of astrology. The author suggests this same viewpoint elsewhere in his account. Because the mountain was of such great altitude in comparison with other mountains in the area, it was considered that its summit supported the entire sky. It was also probably the result of the same fact that it was considered that the science of astrology had been born here, and this in turn suggests that the mountain itself was possibly the site from which astrological observations were made. Indeed, when King Hesperus ascended its summit only to be swept away by strong winds, he had done so to observe the stars. Perhaps the altitude of the mountain made the skies all the more clearer from its summit, facilitating a better observation of them? It is also stated that the spherical nature of the heavens had been discovered upon the mountain which perhaps suggests that the precise shape of the Earth had been visible from its summit. If such forms of knowledge had been possessed by the Atlantians, then this also would imply a higher degree of cultivation and technological development amongst them.

A further author who speaks of Lake Tritonis as well as Mount Atlas is Herodotus. His Histories, written in the 5th century B.C., take the form of an historical survey of the various parts of the globe surrounding the central theme of the epic battles fought between the Greeks and the Persians. Much of the detail of this survey, however, is slightly less than reliable, and because of this takes on a rather legendary character. In Book IV the author discusses the various peoples of Libya and their particular customs, and it is this particular section that is of interest to us.

Herodotus informs us that along the coastline of Libya from Egypt, a people called the Machlyes were found, who, like their neighbours the Lotophagi, made prolific use of the lotus fruit. As well as eating it they also brewed their wine from it. Their land bordered a sizeable river known as Triton which in turn ultimately led to a vast lake called Tritonis. Within this lake an island was found which they called Phla and an oracle once stated that the Lacedaemonians should one day attempt to settle here.

Herodotus also takes the opportunity to tell us a little about the story of Jason and the crew of the Argo which is at a slight variance to other accounts of the same story. Having set off towards Delphi the crew were caught in strong winds and blown towards Libya. Apparently before they knew what had happened, they had run aground in the shallow waters of Lake Tritonis. At a loss as to what to do, luck had it that Triton himself appeared, carrying his trident. In return for a bronze tripod Jason had brought with him, Triton promised to show him and his crew the way out of the lake. When he had received this gift, Triton uttered a prophecy to the effect that when the descendants of the crew of the Argo returned to steal the tripod, a hundred Greek cities should be built along the shores of Lake Tritonis. When the local populace of the region heard of this, however, they quickly hid the tripod to ensure that none should ever find it.

Returning to the tribes people of the area, Herodotus next describes the Auses. This people were immediately adjacent to the Machlyes, and also lived upon the shores of Lake Tritonis, the river forming a natural division between them. Unlike the Machlyes who were in the habit of letting their hair grow long at the back, the Auses let it grow long at the front. Each year they held a festival in honour of their patron goddess Athena and the young girls of the tribe would gather to fight with sticks and stones. The custom was said to have had its origins in the most ancient of times. It was also said that if any of the girls was mortally wounded during the enactment of these rites, then it was as a direct result of her lack of chastity. Immediately before the actual fight, a girl was chosen with the most favourable looks and dressed in Greek armour complete with helmet. She was then placed in a chariot and driven around the lake. It was a matter of speculation as to precisely how the girl was dressed before Greek speaking people arrived at the area, but it is possible that the armour had previously been native African or even Egyptian. It was also maintained by the Auses that Athena had been the daughter of Poseidon and had been born from Lake Tritonis itself. After an argument with her father, however, she had instead been adopted by Zeus who took her as his own.

In describing the peoples that lived to the south along the sand belt stretching from Thebes to the Pillars of Heracles, the Ammonians are first mentioned followed by the Garamantes. It was this latter tribe who were the closest to the Lotophagi. Next after the Garamantes came the Atarantes. Immediately adjacent to them was a stretch of rough terrain that eventually led to the slopes of Mount Atlas itself. The mountain apparently had steep conical sides to it which rose to such a height that the mountain's summit was almost perpetually hidden by cloud. The people inhabiting the region were known as the Atlantes but they mountain itself they called 'the Pillar of the Sky'. The people were avid vegetarians which they claimed aided them with their sleep in the hot climate.

This is the sum of what Herodotus tells us of the various tribes people that dwelt within the region of Lake Tritonis and Mount Atlas. From the fact that the author clearly names the island in Lake Tritonis as Phla, that he is referring to an entirely different age to the one Diodorus Siculus was speaking of; indeed, it was an age that was entirely contemporary with his own. In Diodorus it had been called Hespera, as we have said possibly after the king who had originally ruled it, but since then it had been conquered both by the Amazons and then the Greeks with the assistance of Perseus and Heracles. As a direct result of this of course it is entirely possible that the island had been renamed, having been inhabited by an entirely different people.

But if the islands of Phla and Hespera were indeed one and the same, how could this have been so if the lake it was contained in, Tritonis, had entirely disappeared during the course of an earthquake? As has been stated earlier, perhaps the factors that had led to the lake's disappearance had been far from permanent? If the water courses that fed the lake, for example, had been diverted, causing it to dry up for a number of years, then it is quite possible that at a later time, perhaps after the passing of some years, the basin it had been contained in was simply refilled. Of course, by then the people living in the area were of an entirely different character and had renamed the island. However, to Greek speaking people, the main lake still retained its original name, having been recorded in their history books that way.

The tribes people who lived immediately adjacent to the Machlyes and the Auses, and who also dwelt on the shores of Lake Tritonis, are rather intriguing. As their name 'Lotophagi' suggests, their chief source of sustenance was the lotus fruit. Today it is generally considered that the lotus in question was actually the jujube tree which produces a dark red, date-like fruit and is still often used as a source of food. However 'lotus-eaters' are also mentioned elsewhere in Greek mythology such as in Homer's Odyssey when the hero and his men encountered them after having been blown off course in a gale. As they had been forced southwards from the Cape of Malea, the land they had arrived in could well have been Libya. After having consumed some of the fruit the local populace in the area were in the habit of eating, which had the effect of producing a rather dreamy state of contentment, his men had refused to return again. In the end Odysseus was obliged to use force.

Homer describes the fruit in question as being sweet and 'flowery' in taste, and one wonders whether or not this lotus had not actually been a flower. Indeed one example of a lotus flower that was actually eaten for its various 'medical' properties is the Egyptian lotus. This was a lily native to the Nile Valley which was very much venerated by the Egyptians being considered a cure-all. It was used for such wide and varied purposes as for the manufacture of perfumes, and its flowers when eaten had a mild tranquillising effect. Indeed Herodotus himself actually states elsewhere that the 'lotus' was sometimes eaten in ancient Egypt because of these properties.

Could this have been the same plant consumed by the Lotophagi? It is tempting to believe that it could have been as the people in question lived not that far from a large river and lake and so therefore could well have been the same species as the Egyptian lotus. Perhaps the plant had also grown in profusion in the waters of the river and lake to be regularly gathered by the people who inhabited its shores. One objection to this however is the observation that Herodotus states that the Lotophagi had not lived immediately adjacent to the river and lake in question, as the Machyles had dwelt immediately between this tribe and the Triton. Indeed, he goes on to inform us that the Machyles ate less of the lotus than the Lotophagi did. However the possibility that the fruit in question was actually the Egyptian lotus is still an interesting one.

Although Herodotus is comparatively brief in his description of Mount Atlas and its immediate environs, what he does tell us is extremely interesting. For example we are told what exactly the mountain looked like and more importantly it is inferred that such a mountain did exist beyond pure myth and legend. Of the inhabitants who live in its vicinity we are told that they were named after the mountain and were called the 'Atlantes'. This name is remarkably reminiscent of the 'Atlantians' of Diodorus and the 'Atlantis' of Plato. It is also interesting that the mountain was referred to as 'the Pillar of the Sky', implying that it was considered to support the sky.

Herodotus also gives clues as to the precise whereabouts of Mount Atlas within the continent of Africa. However his description of its geographical location is still not exactly clear. For example he does not make it precisely clear how great a distance Mount Atlas was from Lake Tritonis and its river. However Herodotus does tell us that the Garamantes, who dwelt along the sand belt which stretched from Thebes to the Pillars of Heracles, were some thirty days travelling from the Lotophagi. And in addition to this, the Garamantes were ten days distant from the Atarantes, who themselves were only ten days away from the slopes of Mount Atlas. As the distances quoted appear to be in the same direction, this would mean that the Lotophagi were only some ten days from the inhabitants of Mount Atlas. Assuming a day's journey to be 15-20 miles, this would have meant that the distance between the two peoples could have been anywhere between 150 and 200 miles.

Of course if this was the case, then this would inevitably have meant that the two kingdoms originally ruled over by the Amazons and the Atlantians would have been of quite some sizeable proportions. But is such a picture that unrealistic given the importance that is given to the two tribes in question?

In general, therefore, the more contemporary picture described by Herodotus very much confirms the far older, legendary one given by Diodorus. In both accounts Lake Tritonis is fed by a large river called Triton and not too far away is a tall, steep-sided mountain called Atlas. Again, the lake has an island in it of significant size, though in Herodotus the name given to this is quite different. The latter author also confirms that Greeks had visited the region in the distant past and indeed that there was even a further prediction to the effect that they would visit the area in the future as well.

Another interesting detail revealed by Herodotus was the custom present among the Auses of holding a festival each year in honour of Athena. Among the Greeks the latter had very much been a warrior who had offered both protection and her patronage to the people of Athens. Images of her show her with shield and helmet revealing her more feminine or passive role in the art of war—that is, her role as protectress. However there are other aspects of her attire that are of interest to us, and one of these is the aegis that she wore. Decorating this, with the intention of striking terror into the hearts of her enemies, was the head of Medusa complete with its crop of snakes. Athena had apparently been given this as a trophy by Perseus upon his return from Libya.

In addition to this Athena also bore a number of epithets and one of these was 'Tritogeneia'. The latter had been frequently used by the poets such as Homer and Hesiod. Some have interpreted this as perhaps meaning 'thrice born' or 'third born', but this does not necessarily accord with the myth of Athena's birth. The story goes she had been born without a mother, having burst forth from the very forehead of Zeus. However, in the account given by Herodotus of the various traditions held by the Auses, an alternative origin of her epithet is alluded to. The author states that prior to her adoption by Zeus, she had actually been born from the waters of Lake Tritonis itself, her original father having been Poseidon. Although this story refers to the Libyan Athena rather than the Greek one, one wonders whether this had been the origin of her epithet Tritogeneia; literally 'born from the Triton'?

In the legends of Perseus and Heracles it is apparent that there was a tradition of Greek-speaking people having visited the region many years previously. Had this been how the Auses had obtained their peculiar custom of dressing a young maiden in Greek armour and driving her around the lake? Herodotus specifically states that the style of armour worn by the ceremonial maiden had very much been Greek in character and even goes so far as to claim that the helmet had been Corinthian. The author was also of the opinion that the custom of dressing in this manner had been the direct result of Greek settlement in the area. However, if the custom of the Auses had come about as the direct result of a cultural interchange, which way around exactly had it been? Had Athena actually been Tritonian in origin and had then set out for Greece, or had the Athena of the Auses originally been a Greek traveller? Whatever Athena's precise origins were, it appears that Greek-speaking people had still possibly visited the region some time long ago.

Another interesting fact is the circumstance that it is Athena who bears the head of the Gorgon upon her breastplate, even though it was actually Perseus who had travelled to Libya to obtain it. Of course the reason for this was that the latter had given it to Athena as a trophy. However knowing that Athena could well have been born in Lake Triton, could it not have been the case that she was based upon an original Amazon prototype? Of course, if Athena had been an Amazon, then the title of Tritogeneia would have been highly apt as it was within Lake Tritonis that the Amazons had dwelt. Perhaps the figure in question upon whom the Greek Athena had been based was Myrina herself as a result of the many victories she had won on behalf of her tribe.

Indeed as it was the latter who had originally defeated the Gorgons, it would only have been appropriate for her to have worn the head of their queen, Medusa, upon her breastplate. Whatever the case however, at the end of the day it must have been a temptation for the Greeks, when they had first encountered these female warriors, to see in them an ideal which they subsequently made their own.

Herodotus also briefly mentioned the story of the voyage of the Argo as an example of how Greek-speaking people had arrived in the area. The fuller account of the story given by Apollonius of Rhodes, again has the crew of the Argo being blown off course in strong gales. However on this occasion they are carried some way inland over shallow waters as a result of a storm surge. Having finally come to rest on dry land, they realise they are confronted by desert in every direction in front and unnavigable waters behind. The crew receive an oracle however and, following the directions given by it, carry their boat further inland. Having undertaken this arduous task for nine days, they finally arrive at Lake Tritonis.

Near the lake they stumble upon the very place where the serpent had guarded the golden apples as well as the Hesperides, who were still close by bewailing the loss of their fruit. When the Argonauts approached them however, they instantly turned to dust. Once they had launched their ship onto the lake, the crew set sail to find a way out. After a day's navigation they had still not found an outlet and so made ready to make an offering of a bronze tripod to its waters. At the very same moment Triton himself appeared and pointed out a way that eventually led to the sea. The crew followed this until they came to the coastline and from here it was only a short distance to Crete.

If the geographical details of Apollonius' quite obviously fictional account can at all be relied upon, it would appear that the lake in question was of appreciable dimensions for the crew of the Argo to have sailed around it for an entire day without finding an outlet? It would also appear that the lake must have been deep enough to have sailed in without hindrance, though Herodotus does inform us that the Argo had actually become stuck in shallow waters at one point and that this was why Triton had stepped in to help them out. But presumably, however, they were free to sail as they pleased after this, having been shown a course which eventually led them out from the lake.

However one important difference between Apollonius' story and the picture as it has emerged so far, is that the river Triton actually flowed out of the lake rather than into it. Both Diodorus and Herodotus inform us that the lake had been fed by this river but, in Apollonius, it quite clearly flows *out* of the lake and into the sea. In this regard it would appear that it was the lake that was the source of the river rather than the river the source of the lake.

A further point apparently cleared up by Apollonius is the precise location of the garden of the Hesperides in relation to Lake Tritonis. The author clearly places this garden immediately adjacent to the shores of the lake, meaning that perhaps we had been correct in assuming that as the island in the lake had been called Hespera, the garden of the Hesperides must have been present either upon the lake in question or within a close proximity to it.

In summary, therefore, it would appear that legends relating to Mount Atlas and the lake near to it, Tritonis, were quite prevalent throughout Greek mythology and were not just confined to the writings of Diodorus. Such stories may well have referred to actual geographical features, though their precise whereabouts is, of course, open to debate. It is possible that these features had been located at the very periphery of the known world of the time and that the stories about this land were inevitably exaggerated and distorted as a result of their constant retelling. However, for the time being we will put aside any discussion on the precise whereabouts of the land in question until we return to this theme in the closing chapter.

4

In Egyptian Myth and Legend

It has been made quite apparent that the story of Atlantis as told by Plato, had originally issued from the land of Egypt before being passed onto his great grandfather by Solon. Because of this, it would appear that, before arriving in Greece, the myth had been current in Egypt as well. However, how accurately this story had been retold by Plato is, of course, as has already been discussed in chapter one, entirely open to debate. On a purely factual basis it can quite clearly be shown that Plato had at the very least been rather less than accurate, which rather suggests he had somewhat embellished the story with his own imaginations.

But upon further reflection to what extent can such idiosyncrasies be put down to Plato as an author or to the fact that the story he had retold was actually Egyptian in origin? In other words, to what extent had the story differed in the first place before being received by Solon? It is likely that we shall never know the answer to this for sure and, in any case, judging by his performance elsewhere, it is apparent that Plato was in the habit of spinning a bit of a yarn now and then. Nevertheless, it is still a possibility that the myth that had been current in Egypt had differed in one or two key respects from the legend as recounted by Diodorus.

Indeed it is fairly apparent that not ever fact and figure that is quoted by Plato is a complete fabrication, as other Greek authors testify that such a mythological tradition had existed in ancient Egypt. Herodotus, for example, claimed that the Egyptians could trace their history back many thousands of years prior to the Greeks during which time there had been at least four world-changing events. The cause of these catastrophic events apparently being a radical shift in the sun's position in the sky. This offers a striking parallel to part of the story outlined at the beginning of the Timaeus in which the myth of Phaëthon is described. And again, as with Plato, Herodotus claimed that for some unique reason the land of Egypt had been entirely unaffected by these catastrophes and had continued to prosper.

Herodotus reports that the actual time period involved in which the Egyptians claimed they could trace back their history, amounted to some 341 generations. The author, assuming three generations to be equivalent to a hundred years, calculated this period as having a span of some 11,340 years. Of course, this is no modest figure and is not too dissimilar from the 9,000 years quoted by Plato. Indeed, if the exact number of years to a generation had been slightly overestimated by Herodotus, then 341 generations could easily have been the exact equivalent of 9,000 years.

Another author to take a keen interest in the many customs and beliefs of the Egyptians, was Diodorus. Like Plato and Herodotus, he too commented upon the huge length of time over which the Egyptians claimed to have traced their history. However this author was of the contrary opinion that these figures were entirely unrealistic and were probably more the result of the differing methods of reckoning time. According to Diodorus the Egyptian priests claimed their records went back some 23,000 years, a figure even larger than that found in Plato or Herodotus. This however, also included the reigns of the various divine beings who ruled Egypt immediately prior to the first of the pharaohs. Diodorus concluded that such a large figure had been the direct result of the reckoning of time by the lunar month which has a duration of course of thirty days. If this had been the case, then this would give us the actual number of nearly 1,900 years. This is a somewhat more realistic figure especially if it is considered that the first of the pharaohs of Egypt is thought to have reigned sometime around 3,000 B.C.

Diodorus goes on to quote a further example of how the Egyptians had apparently been in the habit of overstating the number of years that had passed by. In stating the reignal years of some of their pharaohs, a figure of 300 was not uncommon and this, of course, is completely unrealistic. The explanation the author gives for this, and which is also the answer that was suggested in chapter one, is that in this particular instance the Egyptians had used the seasons for the reckoning of time. As there had been three seasons in each Egyptian year, this would give a reignal period for the upper figure of 100 years. This, although far more realistic, is also a rather generous figure.

Another point that is worth noting in connection with the exact time periods that are quoted by Plato, is that in some respects the account he gives of them is rather contradictory. The Egyptian priest who delivered the story to Solon was at pains to point out that the institutions of Egypt only went back some 8,000 years. Of course, if their institutions only went back so far, then how was it possible that they could have records of events that had occurred 1,000 years before this, that is 9,000 years previous? We can only assume that the history in their possession was rather vague and legendary, and that the time period involved had consequently perhaps been overestimated.

A similar picture is implied in Diodorus, even though it is actually the Amazons rather than the Atlantians who challenge the Greeks, that the events in question occurred many years before the founding of Egypt. Indeed Myrina, the Amazon queen who had been responsible for leading her people into Asia Minor, had first formed a treaty with Horus who was then the reigning pharaoh of Egypt. Since Horus is an entirely mythical figure and also a divinity among the ancient Egyptians, we can only assume that Diodorus had been implying that the events in question had taken place quite some time before the founding of pharaonic Egypt, that is when the divine beings had ruled the land.

Indeed, the forming of a 'treaty' as such between Myrina and Horus is more than likely at least in part a story, as the various peoples living in the region at the time were probably not that highly ordered or indeed that centralised anyway. It is more than likely that the Amazons would have been granted a free passage in any case. However, there is also the possibility that the treaty referred to another set of events which offered a striking parallel. Since the Amazons had settled in parts of Asia Minor, especially along the courses of rivers having themselves originated from a land that was watered in the same way, perhaps they had also settled along the course of the Egypt's river, the Nile? Having encountered little resistance from the local populace upon entering the land, such must surely have been a temptation?

If this had been the case, then perhaps the memory of these fearsome women could be found in the figure of Neith, the Egyptian warrior goddess. Although strictly speaking the exact role of the latter is open to debate, it is clear that she possessed a pronounced warrior side to her as the symbols related to her were a shield and a pair of crossed arrows. Like the Greek Athena, had Neith also been modelled on an Amazonian prototype? It is also the case that a number of the queens from the first dynasty bore the name Neith, which perhaps suggests the divinity in question had been based upon a real individual who had once performed the role of queen. Many of the early male pharaohs bear the name of Horus in memory of the legendary first king of Egypt, so it is only natural to assume that perhaps Neith had been a first queen? When Diodorus stated that a treaty had been drawn up between Myrina and Horus, had this treaty also included a marriage between the Egyptian king and the Amazon queen? Indeed Diodorus does indeed suggest that some sort of 'friendship' had existed between the two but does not specifically mention marriage. If this situation had been the case, then it is also highly likely that there had been at least some accompanying settlement in the area by this tribe of women.

Considerations such as these also very much raise the issue of the precise origins of the Egyptians themselves and their pharaonic line. It has always been a bit of a mystery as to how exactly such an ancient and complex civilisation had come about, apparently generating completely of its own accord, and there are a number of possible explanations for this. One of these which has already been raised, is the intervention of a slightly older civilisation such as that found in Mesopotamia. A process of evolution through cultural influence being suggested. However, by far the more popular is the suggestion that such a development is purely the result of geographical locality. Again using Mesopotamia as a prime example, civilisation prospered in the flood plain of a large river, or rivers, which supplied fertile soils and irrigation for crops. These may well indeed have been the essential ingredients which allowed civilisations to prosper. Having accepted this however, it is still a mystery as to where exactly the people concerned who originally embarked upon this endeavour had emanated from and what caused them to experiment in this particular area in the first place? Again, this leaves open the possibility of cultural influence though combined geographical good providence.

Among the ancient Egyptians themselves their exact origins was also the subject of much mythological speculation. Before the first pharaohs, a number of divine ancestors were said to have ruled for a period spanning many centuries. Indeed similar beliefs are found among many primitive cultures where it is known as ancestor worship. Foremost among these divine ancestors, and who also became, at least in symbolic form, the first pharaoh of Egypt, was Osiris. Indeed it was the latter who had taught the Egyptian people the art of cultivation and was also therefore their first great civilizer. His reign, however, came to an abrupt end when, according to legend, he was murdered by his evil brother Seth. In vengeance for his death, his son Horus set out to regain control of the land and destroy the evil Seth. This archetypal struggle between Horus and Seth has been interpreted by many as a struggle between the two rival powers of Upper and Lower Egypt in pre-dynastic times. Presumably whoever had won this battle became the ruler of the two lands. It is quite likely that the double crown worn by many of the pharaohs, which consisted of the white crown of Upper

Egypt and the red crown of Lower Egypt, had commemorated this unification.

But was the figure of Osiris in any way based upon an actual historical figure who had brought the knowledge of art of cultivation to Egypt? Diodorus had much to say on the matter and collected together a number of myths on this subject. Apparently Osiris had been the original founder of Thebes, a city located some way up the Nile from the delta. Here gold and copper had been mined that had been used in the manufacture of implements for hunting and cultivation. On the instruction of Osiris all of the land surrounding the city had been turned over to farming. The king then raised an army for the specific purpose of bringing civilisation to the other parts of Egypt as well. These events, so Diodorus claims, occurred some 10,000 years ago, though some have stated that this had actually been some 23,000 years.

Elsewhere, Diodorus relates the theory that the Egyptians had actually been a colony of Ethiopians whose leader had been called Osiris. Apparently the story goes that many years ago the land of Egypt had not yet formed itself properly but was instead covered by sea. After many years of alluvial deposition laid down by the Nile, land was eventually created. Having observed the fertility of this land, the Ethiopians set out to inhabit it. It is by virtue of this fact that many of the customs held by the Egyptians bear a striking resemblance to those found in Ethiopia. Both of these people for example consider their kings as divine and give great importance to their burials. The style of their statuary is also apparently very similar, as is the writing they use. Of the latter, the Ethiopians, like the Egyptians, make use of two types of lettering, that which is used by the people, 'demotic', and that used by the priests, 'hieratic'. The various observances of the priests are also similar between both peoples, as is the manner in which the kings dress themselves.

How much substance there actually was to this suggestion and how much of it was pure speculation on Diodorus' part, we cannot tell; but at least we have a story which gives credence to the idea that the Egyptians had their own traceable origins. Precisely how long the Nile valley had been in a habitable condition before people began to arrive is one issue that is not covered by Diodorus. Presumably, as the flood plain surrounding the river became inundated with rich alluvial soil deep enough to grow crops in, the first settlers began to arrive. Whether this had been a gradual process or had happened all at once under the leadership of a ruler called Osiris, is, of course, open to debate and depends upon how literally the stories related can be taken.

An interesting observation to be made about Diodorus' account is the fact that the settlers of the Nile valley came from a southward direction, Ethiopia lying almost due south of Upper Egypt. In fact, the Nile has part of its source in these lands, the Blue Nile cascading down from the highlands of Ethiopia. Having the source of such a large river in a close proximity to one's lands must have the cause of much temptation to explore further downstream? Indeed, such explorations must have occurred many times over in the distant past until it was eventually discovered that the alluvial soils of the Nile Valley were fertile enough to support an abundance of plant life. Having made such a discovery, perhaps it had been decided upon by a local leader that a migration of people should occur along the course of this river so as to settle this rich and fertile land. Had this ruler perhaps been called Osiris and had he overseen the introduction of the cultivation of crops here? Such a scenario is not that implausible.

This picture would also raise a further question which is what part of the Nile Valley exactly had these colonists originally settled in, as the Nile Valley is vast and covers many hundreds of miles? Presumably as a result of the fact that the Blue Nile joins the White Nile some way upstream, these colonists must have encountered an abundance of fertile land here before arriving anywhere near the delta region. Because of this it would appear likely that the colonists would first have settled in the lands of Upper Egypt. Indeed, the crown that is worn by Osiris, the ruler of these people, has always been the tall, white crown of Upper

Egypt. In addition, his cult centre and assumed burial place at Abydos, is also very much within the lands of Upper Egypt.

Of course if this had been the situation, then this would also have meant that the people of the delta region, the land of Lower Egypt, if there had been any around at that time, would have been represented by an entirely different race of people. Assuming that the two peoples did not exactly see eye to eye, perhaps this was the reason for the division of the land into two rival, warring kingdoms, that of Lower and Upper Egypt? Certainly the existence of a separate crown for each kingdom, the red and the white crowns, would surely suggest that two entirely different peoples had originally inhabited these lands?

As each of these nations developed and also expanded, it was inevitable that they would eventually war over lands at the very boundary between the two kingdoms. Perhaps their rivalry had developed to such an extent that a conquest took place by one of the nations to obtain ultimate power over both Upper and Lower Egypt. In the story of the contention of Horus and Seth after the murder of Osiris by Seth, was there not a remembrance of this ultimate struggle between the rulers of these two lands? Versions of the story do have Horus and Seth controlling each of the two lands, with Horus intending to take the lands of Seth in revenge for the murder of his father. However, rather than a battle taking place between two rival armies, the matter is settled in the form of a series of contests between Horus and Seth in person—the winner being judged by Ra himself.

It is obvious that the story in content is largely a myth. Indeed if Horus and Seth had been so closely related, being depicted as nephew and uncle or sometimes as brothers, then how could they have ruled over two entirely distinct lands? In any case, the settling of the matter of who the ultimate ruler should be through a series of contests, is quite plainly out of the question. Seth himself is obviously a mythical figure as he has a number of bestial attributes to him and also came to represent chaos and disorder. However, there is at least some resemblance to history in the story in the fact that Osiris, who wears the white crown, appears to have been the ruler of Upper Egypt, whereas his son, Horus, the unifier of the two lands, wears the double crown of the red and white crowns combined.

So if Osiris had been the ruler of Upper Egypt and Horus the ruler of the two lands combined, then who had been the original ruler of Lower Egypt? It is obvious that Seth, as we have already stated, is largely a mythical figure who came to represent everything malign and evil, and because of this is more than likely a creation of the storyteller. Images of him also do not show him as wearing any crown of sorts, his tall horn-like ears presumably precluding the possibility anyway. Of course as the ruler of Lower Egypt he would have worn the red crown which is flat on the top with a back to it giving it a rather chair-like appearance. Having identified Osiris as the wearer of the white crown and Horus the wearer of the double crown, which particular figure is closely associated with the red crown? As has been mentioned earlier, it is the goddess Neith who is closely identified with the Nile Delta, and hence Lower Egypt, and because of this is depicted as wearing the red crown. Had this been the mythical ruler of this land at the time when Osiris had ruled in Upper Egypt?

As already stated it had been the custom among the first dynasty rulers to name their queens after Neith while the kings on the other hand had been named after Horus, the unifier of the two lands. Perhaps there was some logic to this? As the son of Osiris, the original king of Upper Egypt, Horus had initially represented a rival of Neith, the queen of Lower Egypt. However to enable the two lands to combine, wouldn't it have been appropriate for the son of the king of Upper Egypt to have married the queen of Lower Egypt? Such an arrangement would have been advantageous in the fact that two distinctly separate peoples were now merging into one larger power.

So if the people of Upper Egypt had originated from a land far to the south towards the source of the Nile, such as Ethiopia, then where had the people of the delta region come from? As has been discussed earlier, as Neith had been a warrior queen, perhaps it was possible that she and her people had been Amazons who had settled in the area while the rest of the tribe had been making their way into Asia Minor? Having previously inhabited a watery region in the form of an island in a large lake, perhaps the delta had offered an ideal environment in this respect with its yearly floods and numerous islands of dry land?

The myth of the murder of Osiris tells us that after he had been slain by Seth, his body suffered the fate of dismemberment, the various parts being scattered all over the lands of Egypt. This fate was particularly objectionable to the Egyptians who lay special emphasis on proper burial custom. However Isis managed to gather together all these body parts and being versed in the healing arts, shaped the first mummy. It was from the last remnants of life still present in the mummy, that Isis was able to conceive the child Horus, the future king of Egypt. After the latter had succeeded in avenging his father by banishing the evil Seth, Horus was made the earthly king while his father, Osiris, became the king of the underworld. Here the latter very much continued with his previous role as ruler and images show him as seated on a throne holding the royal crook and flail and adorned with the 'atef' crown, the latter consisting of the white crown with a plume on either side of it. Osiris was also represented in mummiform, and in Egyptian burial custom when the deceased was prepared for burial, it was considered that he was dressed in the manner of Osiris.

This story of Osiris had very much shaped the Egyptian view of the afterworld. To the Egyptians, death represented the beginning of a second existence in which the individual joined with Osiris to dwell in his kingdom. However to join Osiris in his abode meant first journeying along an often hazardous route in order to arrive there. The deceased however, was not unassisted in this task, as placed alongside him in the funerary chamber was the Book of the Dead. It was this latter document, written on a scroll of papyrus and which contained both images and text, that listed many spells and prayers intended to guide the deceased on this often hazardous journey to the afterworld. Any dangers encountered along the way were overcome with the appropriate spell and offering.

Contained in the Book of the Dead are a number of chapters, each of which depict the various stages in the journey until the eventual arrival in the afterworld. The remaining chapters depict the life the deceased is expected to live once he has arrived there. It appears that the Egyptians considered the afterlife to be very much a mirror image of the everyday world with the deceased carrying out much the same activities as he had in his previous existence. Indeed, the texts often refer to his ability to enjoy such pleasures as drinking beer and eating cake and there are even images of him playing draughts.

In the opening chapters the deceased's mummy is shown as being drawn along in a funerary boat accompanied by some of his worldly goods. Ultimately the procession leads to a tomb where the curious 'opening of the mouth' ceremony is performed. It was this ceremony that was said to have restored life to the mummy; hence allowing him to continue on his journey. Before setting out, however, the deceased has to acknowledge certain recognisable features, and the first of these is the Nile itself, represented as a seated man coloured in blue. This is followed by a figure called the 'Great Green Lake' who has his hands outstretched over two lakes of natron and nitre and beside this appears 'Restau', the gateway of the afterworld.

After this there follows a series of spells which allow the deceased to overcome each of the obstacles on the way to the afterworld and these are represented in the form of a series of pylons, each of which is inhabited by its own guardian. As for the journey itself, the chief means of transport appears to have been by boat which is powered by two oars towards the rear. Indeed, the sled used to transport the mummy of the deceased to the tomb at the very beginning of the papyrus is also a boat of the same design. It would appear therefore that a large part of the journey was to take place by water and that the afterworld itself lay on the other side of a large expanse of water.

After a series of litanies to the numerous divine beings who oversaw the various parts of the afterworld and a number of spells that enabled the deceased to 'live and breath' in this land, he finally arrives at his intended destination. Sometimes described as the Field of Offerings or Field of Reeds, the deceased commences to plough and reap and indulge in all the earthly pleasures he is so used to. Having previously been a Ba spirit, the ordinary, everyday soul of the deceased representing his personality and which was depicted as a bird with a human head, he is now transformed into a Khu, that is, an immortal being living in a state of perfect contentment.

However, there is one immediate peculiarity about this Field of Reeds or Offerings, and that is that the land in question appears to be surrounded on all sides by water. The fields in question therefore would appear to be a series of islands, or at least a single island accompanied by several smaller ones. In between the images of the deceased ploughing and reaping in this land, boats feature quite prominently and the deceased is shown as rowing one in order to meet one of its rulers. Another curious feature present upon this island or group of islands, is a staircase-type structure which is also shown inside the boats, one of which is raised upon a column of water. Their precise significance is open to question, but one suggestion is that they represent the 'primeval mound' of Egyptian mythology.

Further confirmation of the fact that we are dealing with an island is found in the fact that a 'Lake of Offerings' also accompanies the land in question. The deceased has first to cross this in order to arrive at the fields. So it would appear that the Field of Offerings is contained within the Lake of Offerings and therefore represents an island of sorts within it. Connected to this lake are a number of waterways and a river is also spoken of. Perhaps this had been the river that supplied the lake or alternatively an outlet along which its waters could flow? However, also present upon the island are a number of cities which further adds to its worldly character. Indeed, one of the towns that is spoken of is apparently populated by fish-worshippers which immediately causes us to think of the Ethiopian Ichthyophages of Diodorus.

This is not all, however, as not far from the lake and island there is a tall mountain called Bakhu. The latter is described as lying in the east which implies that it and the lake lie in an east-west direction. Having been told about its generous dimensions, we are also informed that it was considered that the sky had rested upon its shoulders. However, this is all the texts tell us of the exact nature of the afterworld.

It is clear that the land in question was considered as the abode of Osiris who ruled as its king. In key parts of the journey to this after-world, Osiris is the figure who is addressed by the deceased. Indeed, if we did not know that the destination in question had been the after-world as such, then we might be very much forgiven for thinking that the land spoken of actually existed somewhere upon the globe. Since the life that is lived on this land is rather materialistic in character, then perhaps the landscape itself could also be considered as possessing material substance to it. Perhaps we could suggest that the afterworld itself represented some form of fabled or lost land that the Egyptians, when their lives ended, considered they returned to? Indeed it could be asked why it had to be Osiris, the first king of Egypt, who became lord of the underworld; why had it not been for example some other more specialised divinity? Perhaps simple logic would dictate that the reason for this was because Osiris had already been its ruler from the very beginning and that the underworld represented the legendary home-land that he and his people had originated from? Moreover it is known among primitive peoples that ancestors are often considered as divine, so could it not also have been the case that an ancestral homeland was considered in much the same light?

If such was the case, then the various themes alluded to in the Book of the Dead immediately start to make sense—the journey by boat across an expanse of water, which most likely begins at the banks of the Nile; the arrival at a fertile land of peace and plenty; the transportation of one's worldly goods to enable the continuation of a rather materialistic lifestyle which mirrors one's life before. Why would all this be necessary if the afterworld were a pure abstraction? It also becomes clearer why the production of a mummy was such a necessity. In order to survive the long journey back to the homeland of the ancestors, the corpse needed to be efficiently preserved.

Such a scenario may also be confirmed by the number of souls that an individual was considered to possess in ancient Egypt. The first of these was the Ba, represented in the form of a bird with a human head which was considered to follow the corpse of the deceased and reunite with it every night. The Ka on the other hand, represented the exact double of the individual and came into being at the very moment of his birth. The latter dwelt in the afterworld throughout his lifetime and it was necessary for the Ba to journey there in order to reunite with it. When this had been accomplished, a Khu was created, which was a perfect, immortal being. Of course, for the Ba to reunite with the Ka, it was necessary for the mummy to make the long, hazardous journey to the afterworld, being transported there by boat.

Another detail that is revealing is the manner in which King Osiris is pictured in these funerary texts. Of course, he is always shown in mummiform and crowned either with the white crown of Upper Egypt or more typically with the atef crown. He also carries the royal insignia of the crook and flail which he holds at his breast. However, whether he is seated or standing, it is usually the case that a blue coloured plinth lies immediately beneath him. Often this plinth or box is filled with wavy lines which in other places indicate water. Indeed, a lotus appears to sprout forth from this blue coloured area which again would indicate the presence of water as these particular plants in Egypt only grow in water. It would appear, therefore, as a result of this symbolism, that Osiris had ruled in a land that was very much inundated with water or at least surrounded by water to the extent that it had formed an island. Of course, such a scenario is entirely consistent with the picture we have described so far.

Elsewhere in the cult of Osiris water again recurs as a prominent theme. His main cult centre and where the supposed site of his burial was said to be located, was at Abydos. A number of very early dynastic tombs are found here and one of these, that of king Djer, was once considered to have been the resting place of Osiris. Djer himself was one of the very first rulers of Egypt and had perhaps been the third in line among these early pharaohs. However, also encountered at Abydos is a further curious structure, the Osireion. Constructed from huge granite blocks, the building lies almost completely sunken beneath the ground and is reached via a descending corridor from the temple of Sety I. The structure had apparently been built into the ground so as to make its floor exactly level with the surrounding water table. This is still the case today and as a result of this the basement of the building is entirely flooded. However, at the centre of this flooded chamber is a raised rectangular platform standing just above the water and which is also level with the floor at the bottom of the descending corridor. Upon this platform stand ten huge rectangular columns which support the ceiling. Also in the walls surrounding the chamber are further recesses, totalling seventeen in number, whose precise significance is unknown.

What could the purpose of such an unusual structure have been? It is clear that its builders had gone to great lengths in order to make its floor exactly level with the surrounding water table, and because of this it is apparent that the element of water had been an essential ingredient in the overall function of the building. Some have suggested that the Osireion is far more ancient than the temple of Sety I which dates to the 19th dynasty, as a result of the gargantuan manner in which it has been constructed. However, whether it is an Old Kingdom structure is entirely open to debate.

Along the walls of the descending corridor are various images from the Book of the Dead and, because of this, it has always been assumed that the building was dedicated to Osiris, lord of the underworld. Upon entering the main chamber of the Osireion, however, an obstacle is immediately encountered as between the floor at the end of the corridor and the platform at the centre is a watery moat some ten feet in width. How was it possible to continue any further without causing a splash and disturbing the serene tranquillity of this hidden chamber? One obvious solution is that in the past a small boat had been moored here which enabled those permitted to cross over to the central island. But what had been contained on this central dry area? As it is considered that the building was possibly dedicated to Osiris, perhaps a cult image of him had sat enthroned here? Indeed perhaps the entire chamber was intended to be reminiscent of the underworld and that the cult statue which stood here symbolised Osiris ruling in his abode? Certainly the excerpts from the Book of the Dead on the walls of the descending corridor would indeed suggest an entrance to the underworld. However, also suggested by the latter are the enactment of certain rites or mysteries performed in honour of Osiris. Indeed, such has been suggested by a number of leading authorities.

If the Osireion had been intended to represent the underworld and that a cult statue had stood on the central dry area, then this would lead us to draw several conclusions as to the nature of the Egyptian underworld. The central platform, by virtue of the fact that it was entirely surrounded by water, would very much possess the character of an island, while the cult statue that was housed here would have symbolised the fact that Osiris was considered to have been its ruler. If certain initiates were led down the corridor and then allowed to view inside the chamber once it had been appropriately lit, perhaps they were being shown the future glory promised to them in the afterworld? Whether the chamber had been used for such purposes of initiation and mystery or whether it simply served as a housing place for a cult statue, the precise form that it did take must surely have been decided by the considered nature of the Egyptian afterworld.

However, there are a couple of other features present upon the central platform that are also deserving of attention. The first of these are stone steps at either end of the platform. Had these steps been intended to be functional in any way? It seems unlikely that they had, for whoever descended them would have become fully submerged in twelve feet of water! No other passageways hidden beneath the water would have given them an easy exit from the chamber. It would seem that the steps must have been of symbolic importance but what they had symbolised is a complete mystery. In some ways however they are reminiscent of the steps pictured in the Book of the Dead found upon the island known as the Field of Offerings. These steps also lead nowhere and the fact that they are coloured in blue would indicate that they are watery in nature. Had they perhaps allowed symbolic passage to and from the water by unseen spirits? We shall probably never know the answer to this for certain.

The second curious feature, or pair of features, present on the central island are two pools, one of which is square, the other rectangular. What had been the function of these? Had something been contained or placed within them at some time? In the Book of the Dead, when Osiris is shown enthroned within the underworld, his seat, as mentioned earlier, is shown as supported by a block or plinth of water. Perhaps his cult statue in the chamber of the Osireion had also been positioned in such a manner—that is, over a pool of water? But why the second pool? To answer this we again return to the Book of the Dead. Here a lotus is shown which blossoms forth from the body of water on which Osiris is seated. Supported on the petals of this flower are the four small figures representing the sons of Horus. It is a possibility that such a scene had also been portrayed in the Osireion. Indeed it is not too difficult to imagine in the cool quiet of this hidden chamber, the image of Osiris seated upon his watery throne dimly lit by the flickering torchlight and before him, sprouting forth from the second pool, a bejewelled lotus flower holding forth the four sons of Horus. This most certainly would have been a peculiar and mysterious sight.

At Abydos, an important theme of water is again suggested by a group of twelve boat burials that are found there. These were uncovered in 1991 and are thought to date back to around the first dynasty.

From end to end, each measures some 50 to 60 feet in length and are located not far from the funerary enclosure of king Djer, whose tomb was considered to have been the burial place of Osiris. Each of the buried boats was made of wood which was then encased in brick and finally painted over in whitewashed plaster. The resultant shape of the tombs very much gave the impression that they contained boats and the manner in which they were painted would originally have caused them to stand out proudly from the surrounding sand.

Such a discovery would cause us to speculate as to the reason why these objects had been positioned here in the first place. The immediate answer would appear to be that the boats must have served as symbolic means of transport to the afterworld for the dead king in question. It is known that many worldly goods were buried alongside people of eminence including shabti figures who would act as servants in the afterlife for the individual concerned. It would seem logical therefore that an appropriately generous means of transport would have been required especially in the case of an important king. However this may justify the presence of a single vessel of large proportions but it would not justify the presence of an entire fleet. The burial chamber of king Djer when it had originally been full, if it had indeed been this king for whom the boats were intended, would hardly have been substantial enough to have filled twelve boats of such dimensions. So what had been their precise significance?

An interesting fact about these boat burials is that several of them appear to have a boulder placed at their prows which would appear therefore to have performed the symbolic function of an anchor. If this had been their intended purpose, then such an arrangement would surely suggest that the boats had been moored there after having completed a long journey rather than having been placed there in dry dock for future use. Perhaps this suggestion may also explain their number, that the boats had arrived there as a fleet in very ancient times?

Abydos was very much associated with the cult of Osiris and it is also quite evident that the site represented an ancestral burial ground dating back to the very earliest of pharaonic times. But had there been a deliberate reason for the selection of this particular locality in the first place for such a burial ground? Did the site, for example, possess some peculiar pre-existing connection with the first of the pharaohs of Egypt? If the stories we have been told relating to Osiris are true, then the latter, when he had originally arrived in this land with his fellow colonists bringing with him the knowledge of the cultivation of crops, he must have disembarked at some point along the Nile in Upper Egypt? Had the exact location of this then become a place of significant importance later on in the minds of the Egyptians? Knowing that their forefathers had landed here, perhaps this had been the reason why they had considered it appropriate to bury their early kings at the same place? Perhaps the fleet of boats had also been placed here in commemoration of this same event?

Indeed boat burials are also found elsewhere in ancient Egypt and a good example of this is at the Giza plateau. It is here, of course, that the pyramids of Khufu, Khafre and Menkaure stand. These perpetual enigmas which tower high above the desert sand dominate the entire horizon for miles around. However, not so noticeable and hidden just below ground level, are the remains, or at least the evidence of their prior existence in the form of the pits they were contained in, of a number of large wooden boats. In total five of these pits were uncovered, three of which were found to be empty. Each is located at the base of the Great Pyramid of Khufu, the tallest and perhaps the oldest of the three pyramids.

The boat pits on the eastern side of the pyramid, two of which are found on either side of where the mortuary temple had stood and a further one which lies parallel with the causeway leading to this temple, were all found to be empty. However the two pits on the southern side of the pyramid were each found to contain boats. One of these was excavated in the 1950's and is now on display in the Boat Museum close to where it was found. It is some 140 feet in length and is put together from cedarwood. Complete with oars, it has a rather majestic, if not fully functional, appearance to it. Indeed there is even some evidence to suggest that it may actually have been used for at least a short period of time before its final deposition.

Such discoveries have inevitably led to the suggestion that perhaps the king's body had been carried in one of these boats to its final resting place and that this had been the reason for their burial here. Indeed this may explain the existence of just the one boat beside the Great Pyramid but it does not explain why there are five in number. Moreover this explanation does not account for the complete absence of boats around the two other pyramids at Giza or indeed at any other pyramid found in Egypt.

Another key point which must also be taken into account and which is perhaps difficult to picture today, is that the Great Pyramid had almost certainly stood on its own for a short period of time. Quite how long this was exactly is slightly difficult to assess but certainly between the reigns of Khufu and Khafre there are some eight years which are taken up by Djedefre. Presumably after Khufu had completed his grand task, his successor had wanted to emulate his forerunner and so building work had begun on the second pyramid, or at least so it seemed, almost immediately. However it is probably realistic to assume that the Great Pyramid had been completed sometime prior to the death of Khufu and that Khafre had only commenced the building of his own pyramid once he had fully established himself as pharaoh. Add this to the eight years resulting from the reign of Djedefre and we are perhaps left with a significant period of time.

Upon a close examination it is also apparent that the Great Pyramid as a structure is unique in a number of respects in comparison with its two neighbours. Indeed the briefest examination of its internal structure is enough to convince one of this. While the pyramids of Khafre and Menkaure have hardly any internal structure at all, each of their burial chambers being situated beneath the ground immediately under the structure above, the Great Pyramid on the other hand has a whole series of differing passageways. For example not only does it have both an ascending and descending corridor, but also a tall gallery leading up towards the 'king's chamber'. In addition there is a further 'queen's chamber' which is reached via a level passageway from the ascending corridor as well as a subterranean chamber dug into the ground beneath the pyramid itself. As a result of this it has to be admitted that the Great Pyramid is an entirely unique structure with the two accompanying pyramids being lesser copies of the original.

Another feature which singles out the Great Pyramid as the unique structure that it is, is the fact that it is built immediately above a mound which has been incorporated into its very foundations. Considering that there is evidence of much levelling elsewhere on the plateau, one wonders why the ground here had not been similarly treated in this manner? Indeed, what else are we to conclude but that this natural mound bore some special significance to the ancient Egyptians and that this could possibly explain why the pyramid had been built here in the first place? Could the pyramid above the mound not be considered as a natural extension of the original feature, or in other words an amplification of its overall height?

Long before the Egyptians had even thought of embarking upon their grandest building project, there must have been something that had originally drawn them to this particular site before they commenced their construction. Perhaps this had been the suitability of the site in question, that the ground here served as a firm foundation, or that the drainage had been good? However along the Nile there are many possible locations upon the desert plateau overlooking the valley where pyramids can be built. So what had drawn them to this particular location among the many other choices also available? Indeed there is even evidence of activity at the site as early as the time of the first dynasty which would suggest that the site had been in use for many centuries prior to the building of the pyramids—the latter having been built in Old Kingdom times sometime after 2,600 B.C. during the fourth dynasty.

Had this activity at the site perhaps focussed on some natural feature that was present here such as a mound or dome that was visible on the plateau from the valley below? Indeed, it would appear that a second such feature at the very edge of the Giza plateau had had much the same effect and is encountered to day in the shape of the Sphinx. The latter had apparently been carved from a naturally occurring rocky outcrop which formed the bulk of its head and neck, while the rest of its body was created from a horseshoe-shaped hollow dug out around it. Possessing a human head and a lion's body, the Sphinx however has suffered much from erosion. Even during pharaonic times restoration work was often in progress with further stonework being added to repair the natural damage from weathering.

It is quite apparent however that the head of the Sphinx represents a far later addition as its stonework is in a noticeably better state of preservation than found on the rest of the body. Perhaps the previous head of the figure had cracked and fallen at some point in time and this had warranted its replacement? In fact, it is a possibility that the entire figure had originally been leonine in form as there are various iconographic considerations which point this way. It is known for example that the Sphinx was associated with the sun and its cult temple, immediately adjacent to the figure, was most likely dedicated to this purpose. The main reason why this is thought o be the case is that the Sphinx faces due east and hence looks towards the rising sun. Such figures that look towards or rather guard both the rising and setting sun, are found throughout Egyptian iconography. Indeed in certain chapters of the Book of the Dead they are pictured as two seated lions, one facing to the left and the other to the right. They are considered to represent yesterday and today and between them the sun is shown rising above the horizon. These figures are entirely leonine however, and do not have human heads at all.

Had the Sphinx originally been such a lion that kept guard over the passing of time in this manner? If its head had originally been leonine like its body, then perhaps this fact itself may explain why this part of the figure has not survived intact. The weight of the muzzle combining with heavy erosion perhaps causing a crack to appear which then sheared the rocky at this particular juncture. When restoration work was subsequently commenced it was most likely the vanity of the reigning pharaoh that had decided upon the choice of replacement visage. It was sometime after this that the Sphinx became identified both with the sun as well as the ruling pharaoh. Indeed after this custom had been introduced by Djedefre, the pharaohs were often considered as the sons of Ra, the chief sun-god of Egypt. Coincidently, it was also this pharaoh who had ruled between Khufu and Khafre, the builders of the first two pyramids. It is because of this that it is Djedefre who is largely considered as the pharaoh responsible for placing his facial image upon the sphinx.

It cannot be a coincidence either that it is not just the Sphinx that faces due east but the pyramids also are orientated in this direction. Each of the entrances of the pyramids, their accompanying mortuary chapels as well as their valley temples (the latter two being connected via a causeway) also face towards the east. Because of this could it not be argued that the pyramids themselves, like the Sphinx, are also guardians of the rising sun? Considering that each of their four sides looks out to the four cardinal points, with a greater emphasis being placed on the east, it would appear that the pyramids had perhaps had a solar significance. If this had been the case, then their placement on the west side of the Nile valley could also have been an appropriate choice in this respect.

So if the Giza plateau had originally been selected as a result of its opportune location in addition to the fact that it also possessed peculiar rock formations to it, then the overall plan of the site as it appears today is far easier to comprehend. The first structure to be built right at the edge of the plateau and which is perhaps therefore the very oldest, was the Sphinx. Again perhaps the rock formation concerned had coincidentally had a peculiar shape to it which made it look slightly leonine and which had therefore attracted people's attention to it in the first place. Having been carved into an appropriate shape, the Sphinx also served the purpose of standing guard over the main route-way onto the plateau itself.

Attention then shifted to a second unusual feature present upon the plateau in the shape of a raised mound. It was upon this that the Great Pyramid was constructed, the mound being incorporated into its foundations. After this building was complete, Khafre, a successor of Khufu, decided to build his own pyramid immediately adjacent to that of his predecessor. The next available position on the plateau which would have enabled it to have taken an eastern facing aspect in addition to not making it too distant from the Sphinx at the entrance to the site, is the place where the second pyramid now stands. The valley temple of this pyramid by necessity had to be built immediately adjacent to the Sphinx to its south, which otherwise would have stood in its way, and as a result of this the causeway connected to this temple joins the pyramid at a significant angle. Due to the availability of space the third pyramid, that of Menkaure, had to be built to the south and slightly to the south-west of the pyramid of Khafre. As a result of this all three structures stand in a line that is not quite straight.

But why exactly had this mound at the north-east corner of the Giza plateau on which the Great Pyramid was built been of any interest in the first place anyway? We can only speculate that perhaps this feature, as had been the case with the rock from which the Sphinx had been carved, had borne a passing resemblance to some object that had been of special symbolic significance to the people concerned. If the rock from which the Sphinx was carved had borne a passing resemblance to the head of a lion, is it not logical to assume that perhaps the mound on top of the plateau had been pyramidical in form? As a result of this, as has been mentioned earlier, perhaps the pyramid could be considered as a natural extension of this mound. It is this possibility that also gives us an insight into the precise significance that the pyramid had for the ancient Egyptians.

When viewed from a distance, the overall appearance of the Egyptian pyramid creates a distinct impression upon the observer. Upon the horizon, whether silhouetted against the sun or with the sun shining directly upon them, one might be very much forgiven for mistaking them for mountains. These steep-sided piles of rock which finish at a point, must have represented a mountain in its perfect form. It is true that a cone could rival the pyramid in this particular respect, but then the building of a large conical structure is far more difficult to achieve architecturally. Indeed, who would be prepared to argue that these edifices with all the millions of hours that went into their construction were not actually mountains despite the fact that they were man-made? Had it not been the intention of the Egyptians for these monuments to resemble this natural feature that perhaps had so impressed them?

Having recognised this possibility, perhaps it is easier to see why the Great Pyramid had been built upon the site of a raised mound on the Giza plateau. Had this latter structure not been put there to replace the previous natural, but far more modest, feature? If the Great Pyramid had simply been a continuation in altitude of the original rocky mound, then is it not logical that such a mound in a taller, more extended form warrants being described as a mountain? Egypt, however, is not famed for its mountains and especially for ones with such pronounced peaks to them. So why had an artificial mountain, if it can be described as such, been built here in the first place? Perhaps it had reminded them of their homeland, for example, where such a steep sided mountain complete with a peak to it was found? Having left this homeland, perhaps as the result of some natural calamity, and having arrived in the Nile valley and benefited from its rich, fertile soils, had they not considered it appropriate to make use of their new found wealth to build a replica of the natural feature they had left behind? Indeed, if such had been the case, then surely it is easier to understand why a number of boats of appreciable dimensions had been buried in the immediate vicinity of the Great Pyramid. These must have served to represent the arrival of the ancestors who, having navigated the course of the Nile, landed at certain specific junctures along its fertile valley.

Following the natural shape of a mountain, therefore, the pyramids were built so as to survey the entire horizon. Their four sides were each aligned with the four cardinal points which set them very much within a geographical context. One could look at a pyramid for example and immediately find due north or due south. Their alignment with the rising sun or the east-west axis also very much placed them within a worldly context for, as with many mountains in parts of the globe, the sun itself could be seen to rise and set behind them. Exposed to the various elements of the wind, the rain and the sun these were no ordinary buildings as they had no roofs to shelter them. Also, within their interiors, there were no dividing walls as such enclosing many amply sized rooms, but rather a series of tunnels which gave them a subterranean, almost labyrinthine feel. Entering these pyramids gives the impression of descending into some naturally formed cave system which leads on to further hidden caverns within. Indeed, standing at the very centre of one of these structures causes one to think of the simply massive amount of rock being supported directly above oneself.

A mysterious object associated with the pyramids and also intimately linked with the solar cult found at Heliopolis, is the Beneben stone. It appears that the latter had also been pyramidical in form as was its companion, the 'benbenet', which was placed on the tops of obelisks and also on the pyramids themselves. This stone was associated with the Primeval Mound which played a central part in the Heliopolitan cosmogony. The cult had its origins in the very earliest of times in ancient Egypt not long after unification.

According to this cult, all that had existed at the beginning had been a vast expanse of water called Nun. It was from this water that a mound of dry land arose upon which stepped Atum, the lord of Heliopolis. The latter was equated with the sun and was considered as the creator of all things. Upon this land Atum reproduced asexually giving rise to Shu and Tefnut, the embodiment of dry and moist air.

This pair in turn bore Geb and Nut, the earth and the sky, who themselves went on to produce Osiris, Seth, Isis and Nephthys.

It appears that the Benben was closely identified with this first elevation of land to arise from the waters of Nun. If the stone had been pyramidical in form, then this again would represent, in an ideal geometrical form, a natural rising in the land. Indeed, perhaps it was this fact that would explain the choice of location for the building of the Great Pyramid on the Giza plateau. This outcrop of land, located not that far upstream from Heliopolis, also contained a mound-like form upon it. Had the latter perhaps been identified with the Primeval Mound which had arisen from the waters of Nun? The fact of its having been surrounded by boats would strongly suggest a theme of water as would the raised ceremonial causeway linking together the mortuary and valley temples. After this identification had occurred it was then a question of converting this rocky dome into an ideal form. Of course, this form was that which was already shared by the Benben stone, that of a pyramid.

As was the case with the Great Pyramid itself, it was considered that the Benben stone had captured the first rays of the rising sun each day. Indeed, it was for this very reason that the stone was intimately linked with Atum. However, had the Benben stone actually represented a mountain or an island, or both? As an elevation of land it could well have been either or even a mountain surrounded by a lake. In the Heliopolitan creation myth, Osiris was said to have been born upon this island along with his brother Seth and future consort Isis. And it was this latter group who were said to have populated the future world. But had this been the same land from which Osiris had originally set out from bringing with him the knowledge of the cultivation of the crops to the people of Egypt? If it had, then it would appear that it had also consisted of an island surrounded by a lake which in turn was associated with a mountain. After Osiris had arrived in Egypt bringing his knowledge with him, was it not appropriate therefore that the priests of

Heliopolis should have continued the memory of such an event in the form of a creation myth?

If our reasoning is correct then it would appear that Egyptian mythology had also furnished a story whose content was remarkably similar to the ones recounted by Diodorus and Plato in which an island is surrounded by a lake within a larger continent. Perhaps it could be argued that this resemblance is pure coincidence and is more the product of our own creative reasoning than anything else? But let us not forget that Plato's account of the Atlantis story had first originated from the land of Egypt and so must therefore have been richly infused with its legendary and mythological traditions.

5

Where was Atlantis?

From that given us by Diodorus Siculus it is apparent that the Atlantians had dwelt upon the fertile lands surrounding a large mountain from which they had derived their name. Also, not far away, was an island called Hespera, which was situated within a lake. Quite how far away the latter was from the mountain is open to question, but presumably the distance was great enough such that the extent of the kingdom of the Amazons, who controlled it, did not overlap with that of the Atlantians. It is also apparent that a large river had supplied the lake which bore a name from which the lake's own name was also derived, the Triton. However, whether it was the river which had supplied the lake or the lake which had supplied the river, is again open to debate. Apollonius, in *The Voyage of Argo*, appears to suggest that the latter was the situation as the crew had made their way home again along an outlet from the lake which led to the sea. The sea in question had been the Mediterranean and from here it was only a short stop to their final destination.

However were these geographical features entirely fictitious, or had they in fact existed in some remote region of the globe? It is quite possible that the latter was the case, as Herodotus informs us that in Libya a large lake called Tritonis did exist which was fed by a river called Triton. Also not far from here, the same author claims, there was a tall mountain called Atlas which dominated the entire region. If such features had in fact existed somewhere in Africa, then it must surely be the case that they still survive today? Presumably an exceptionally large mountain would not have weathered away in the few thousand years between the time of Herodotus and the present? However if the mountain in question had been an active volcano, there is always the possibility it had exploded. Plato's account does indeed suggest that Mount Atlas could well have been active in this respect, and in Diodorus' account volcanic activity was certainly present upon the island in Lake Tritonis.

But what of the lake? Had it survived in some form or other, or had it, as Diodorus clearly suggests, entirely disappeared? The latter quite clearly states that it had disappeared during an earthquake and this would tend to suggest that remains of it are not visible today. However, as already stated, it is quite possible that its disappearance, if such had indeed been the case, had only been a temporary effect and that after a short interval of time the water courses eventually found their way back into the hollow again where the lake had originally been situated. In this instance it is highly likely that the lake still survives today in some form or other though, of course, its present appearance is probably very different from that of the distant past. Indeed over the years the water levels of lakes can vary quite dramatically.

So if the story does indeed relate to actual geographical features that still exist today, are they as equally impressive to the modern observer as they would have been to an ancient one? Perhaps the proportions of these features had been vastly exaggerated by the ancient narrators and that the equivalents found today are far humbler in appearance? But Diodorus quite clearly states that Mount Atlas was the tallest mountain of the entire region and Herodotus is also kind enough to inform us that the steep-sided mountain was of such a height that its very summit towered into the clouds. Indeed the latter description would even suggest that the mountain had a pronounced conical shaping to it for what other form would a tall steep-sided mountain take if it weren't surrounded on all sides by other equally tall mountains? Moreover it is this last observation which would point to the fact that the mountain in question had perhaps been a volcano which at the time had been in a state of dormancy.

Whereabouts on the globe then is the exact location for the features spoken of? Diodorus informs us that the land in question was situated not that far from Ethiopia and lay towards the ocean. Indeed, some of the inhabitants of the island Hespera, the Ichthyophages, were described as having been Ethiopian in origin. Since Ethiopia lies on the east coast of Africa with Egypt directly to the north, this would tend to imply that the region in question was situated directly to the south. Unless of course the land located in Egypt itself. The only other regions immediately adjacent to the coast are those to the north of Africa and to the west which of course are some distance from Ethiopia. Such a scenario clearly implies that the term *Libya* had only a very general connotation therefore and was used to describe any of the lands of Africa outside of those specifically found within Egypt and Ethiopia.

It is also stated by Diodorus that the Atlantians had conquered the lands immediately adjacent to them, both to the north and to the west. This in itself would suggest that the land in question must therefore have been located towards the south and the east for such an expansion to have occurred. With the ocean lying directly behind them and with uncharted terrain to their south, the only direction they could have expanded in would have been to the north and to the west as Diodorus does indeed state. This again would tend to place the region to the south of Ethiopia in East Africa.

Having pinpointed the general area therefore where our land must have been situated, all that is left now is to draw a rather broad assumption relating to the manner in which the ancient geographers had drawn their maps. In those days of course, before the discipline had fully developed itself, only the largest and most general features were recorded. This must especially have been the case in regions which were infrequently visited and were located at the periphery of the known world. Because of this, it is perhaps safe to assume that the lake and the mountain which are spoken of were the most noticeable features to be found in the region. Indeed the authors concerned are all unanimous in the opinion that both the lake and the mountain were generously proportioned and dominated the entire surrounding land-scape. Looking on a modern-day map therefore and assuming these features to still be in existence, what geographical features might they have been a reference to?

The most impressive example of a large lake which situated to the south of Ethiopia in East Africa, is Lake Victoria. The latter covers an area of almost 70,000 square kilometres and represents the second larg-est lake in the world. Surely any ancient geographer would unquestion-ably have made a record of its existence had he visited the region and would then have duly reported his observations to his fellow country-men? Could this have been the lake the ancient Greeks had called Tri-tonis? Although there are a number of other examples of large lakes in the region, Lake Victoria is by far the greater.

It is also a fact that Lake Victoria represents one of the chief sources of the River Nile. An outlet on its shores leads directly into the White Nile which eventually joins the Blue Nile some miles later further north. Had this been the same outlet spoken of in *The Voyage of Argo* which eventually joined the Mediterranean many miles to the north? It seems possible and indeed Apollonius of Rhodes actually identifies the Nile in one particular section with the river Triton, stating that this had been the old name for the same river. So if the Triton had actually been the Nile, it is only logical to assume that Lake Tritonis had been Lake Victoria, its source. It would seem therefore that the ancient geographers had indeed recorded the most impressive features they had encountered in this land, simplifying them into the form of a river and lake which bore practically the same name.

If Tritonis was one and the same as Lake Victoria, then it is far eas-ier to understand how the ancestors of the ancient Egyptians had arrived at their the new land, having travelled along the length of the Nile river from its source. As suggested earlier, if the ancestors had been Ethiopian, then they would have needed to have navigated the Blue Nile which has its source in the Highlands of Ethiopia. Assuming, however, that the culture concerned was Atlantian or Amazon, then it is likely that they had navigated the course of the White Nile instead starting out from Lake Victoria. Of course, a number of obstacles would have been encountered along the way in the form of a series of cataracts, but these could easily have been avoided by removing the boats from the water and carrying them the short distances involved.

Having established the identity of the lake, what then of the mountain called Atlas? We have been told that it was by far the tallest mountain in the region and dominated the entire landscape. Knowing that the mountain cannot be that far from Lake Victoria, what candidates are there in the region which might fit this description? There are a series of tall mountains following the chain of lakes from the northern tip of Lake Nyasa to the south to Lake Albert in the north-west. A further sizeable mountain is located to the north-east of Lake Victoria in the form of Mount Elgon in addition to Mount Kenya in the east. However the tallest mountain in the region by far and which is also the tallest in the entire continent of Africa, is Mount Kilimanjaro. The peak of the latter towers to such a height above the surrounding plain that it is continually capped in snow. When viewed from a distance the mountain has a serene grace to it, its sides forming an almost perfect symmetry. The reason both for its pronounced altitude in comparison with the surrounding landscape as well as its unusual shape is the fact that the mountain is undeniably volcanic in origin. Formed some 750,000 years ago, when its activity finally ceased its main peak collapsed into a terrace giving it the characteristic flat-topped appearance we are so familiar with.

Was this therefore the Mount Atlas of the Greeks? The mountain is certainly impressive enough to warrant such a legendary description and it seems almost certain that any ancient visitor to the region would have been equally as impressed by the sight of its snowy summit looming high above the horizon. Indeed it could be argued that its flattened summit very much gives it the appearance of a pillar supporting the sky itself. Being such a unique mountain, any ancient Greek visitor to the region would most certainly have reported its existence to his fellow countrymen where it subsequently became the subject of much myth and legend. By virtue of its being present at the very edge of the known world, it would also have been a highly suitable candidate for the pillar which was considered to have supported the sky. Kilimanjaro is also a good candidate for the Mount Atlas of Greek legend in the fact that it is situated almost due east of Lake Victoria. If the latter had been the site of the island called Hespera, then it would indeed have been the island in the west as far as the inhabitants of the region surrounding the mountain were concerned.

It is possible that Kilimanjaro had also been an inspiration to the ancient Egyptians. As discussed in the preceding chapter, after their journey to the underworld as described in the Book of the Dead, the deceased comes to a land where a mountain lies to the east. The latter was considered to have been of some height and to have supported the sky upon its summit. Assuming that such a mountain had been of a legendary influence to the ancient Egyptians, is it possible that the pyramids of Giza had been fashioned after this same mountain? It has already been convincingly argued that these structures in many respects represent the ideal form of a mountain but in the case of the pyramids of Giza this resemblance may go even further than this. Mount Kilimanjaro is not made up of just the one peak but is actually comprised of three quite separate summits located side by side in a line. The two most important peaks are known as Kibo and Mawenzi, but there is also a third lesser peak on the end called Shira. The reason why the latter is not as well known is because it collapsed into a crater while the other two peaks were still forming. This crater in turn was filled with lava which poured forth from Kibo. In all the central peak Kibo is the highest at around 5,900 m, Mawenzi is the second highest at 5,500 m, and third is Shira at around 5,000 m.

Side by side, therefore, the three peaks bear a passing resemblance to the group of pyramids at Giza. As with the latter structures, the central peak is the tallest with a third, slightly smaller peak on the end. However it must be noted that the superior height of the central pyramid at

Giza, that of Khafre, is only apparent as it was built on slightly raised ground and that the Great Pyramid is actually the tallest architecturally. However perhaps this had been a deliberate ploy on the part of the builders as the relative altitudes of the three structures had perhaps been of some symbolic significance to the ancient Egyptians. Like the three pyramids of Giza, Mount Kilimanjaro also looked towards the sun as it was situated in the east, as far as the inhabitants of the lake were concerned. Perhaps at certain times of the year the sun itself could be seen rising from behind its three summits?

Another interesting feature about Lake Victoria and Mount Kilimanjaro is the immediate environment they are contained in as both are surrounded by a huge system of faults known as the Great Rift Valley. Part of this system forms a huge arc bordering the Congo Basin which is comprised of steep sided valleys and tall mountains. Along this section huge lakes fill the valleys, some of which are notable both for their length as well as their depth. Another section of the Rift Valley runs northward from Lake Nyasa, making its way through central Tanzania, Kenya and Ethiopia. Of course, such a system of faulting has over time given rise to numerous volcanoes, some of which are still active today.

It is because of this that the region is very much an appropriate setting for the seismic event that Diodorus spoke of. Having informed us that there had been volcanic activity on the island Hespera which revealed itself in the form of fiery eruptions, he goes on to state that a significant earthquake had caused the lake to completely disappear. Perhaps the seismic event in question had shifted the water courses which supplied the lake as the land rose and fell, and this had led to the lake's drying? Or alternatively perhaps a volcanic eruption had taken place on the island of Hespera itself? If there had indeed been signs of volcanic activity on the island, then surely this must have meant that the island itself was volcanic in origin? Had the island simply detonated resulting in a boiling inferno of lava and steam ultimately leading to the lake's disappearance? However Diodorus clearly states that the entire region was also torn apart, suggesting that the devastation had been far more widespread. Such would suggest a sudden shift in the earth's crust along much of the fault line's length which would most certainly have caused a series of quite devastating earthquakes.

But whatever the exact situation, it is still highly likely that the body of water called Tritonis is still found today in some form or other even though its extent and overall shape could well have been radically altered. Perhaps the lake in its later form when it eventually refilled is indeed found in the shape of Lake Victoria which today is undeniably a unique geographical feature in its own right? But what about the large island that was said to have been located within the body of water? As far as Lake Victoria is concerned a number of small islands are found dotted around its coastline but none of these are of any significant dimensions. Perhaps when the water levels had been lower in the past some of these smaller islands had joined to form a larger one and this is where the island of Hespera is to be found. But such a suggestion however is complete speculation.

Having examined the terrain enclosed by the Rift Valley system in central East Africa, it would appear that the description of the island of Atlantis given by Plato is in many respects reminiscent of its overall appearance. The hill on which King Atlas built his city and which is the same as our Mount Atlas, was surrounded by a plain which faced the sea. Also surrounding this plain on all sides was a ring of tall steep-sided mountains and from the latter water cascaded which in turn fed into a central, circular system of lakes. The western part of the Rift Valley which borders the Congo has a semicircular, ring-like appearance to it and is made up of tall steep-sided mountains as well as valleys. Enclosed within this feature to the east are the plains of Kenya and Tanzania. Although its shape is more of a semicircle than a rectangle, the topography is remarkably reminiscent of the description that is given by Plato.

There are further similarities as the water of the entire region also drains into a central lake in the form of Lake Victoria. Again, an outlet from the central lake does indeed flow out to the sea, but rather than taking the form of a canal it is actually a river; in this case the longest river that is found in Africa, the Nile. Perhaps it is easier to understand why Plato had claimed that elephants had inhabited this land as the creatures are particularly common in this part of Africa.

It would appear therefore that the story of Atlantis as it has been handed down to us in its many varied and differing forms, does indeed appear to have had specific and hence very real origins to it. It was only inevitable that any such tales filtering through of lands at the very periphery of the known world were correspondingly received with a sense of awe and wonder and hence became clothed in much myth and legend. Of course, if the land in question had also contained unique topographical features, then this also would only have added to such stories. However it would also appear that the main factor that had caused the story of Atlantis to make such an impression in the first place was the very fact that the entire region had been adversely affected by seismic activity. Indeed it was one such event that had led to drastic changes in the immediate environment that in turn most likely had had a detrimental effect on the populations living in the area.

One immediate consequence of this event was that an important food source, in the shape of fishing from a lake, had disappeared over-night, and it was as a result of this, and also partly through fear of further upheavals, that the people of the region had perhaps decided to migrate. Having chosen to settle in other lands, some had perhaps journeyed along the course of the Nile to settle in the fertile lands of Upper Egypt. If they had, then perhaps this was how the Egyptians had come by the story of a lost land, from first hand experience.

As to the precise level of advancement of the Atlantians, we can only say that this part of the story had most likely been exaggerated by Plato. What was more likely the case was that the Atlantians were not that advanced for their time, or as far as the place in which they lived was concerned, but only more so in comparison with the surrounding tribes of the region. Indeed at one point Diodorus clearly states as much (III, 54.2).

What to begin with therefore had been a barely credible story that has been passed off by even the least hardened of sceptics, can at the end of the day perhaps be shown to be grounded on very real, historical events. Of course, as the events in question are so distant in time and the records of them as a consequence being as contradictory as they are, we can never be precisely certain how accurate our history is. Nevertheless, our explanation is still a plausible one and who is to say that events such as these had not occurred at some point in time which, in turn, gave rise to many myths and legends about them?

Perhaps it is also now possible to see exactly how Plato's account of the Atlantis story could have taken shape. Having first heard of this legend via Egypt, it is quite possible that language barriers had first resulted in the distortion of key details of the account. It is also likely that the Egyptians had added a religious significance to the story and that this had only made the tale sound all the more fabulous as a result. In addition the ancient Greeks were also of the custom of replacing foreign sounding names with their own equivalents and in the case of an Egyptian legendary mountain, if it had in fact been Bakhu, the name was replaced by the Greek Atlas. It then only followed that the land held by this divinity was then called Atlantis. It cannot be a complete coincidence that Diodorus had done much the same thing when he had received his own account of this 'lost land' from an entirely different, non-Egyptian source. This then perhaps explains the only too apparent disparity between the two main accounts of the story which are given by Plato and Diodorus.

0-595-66804-6

Printed in the United States
26797LVS00003B/174

9 780595 668045